Historicity of the
Mahābhārata
Evidence of Literature, Art & Archaeology

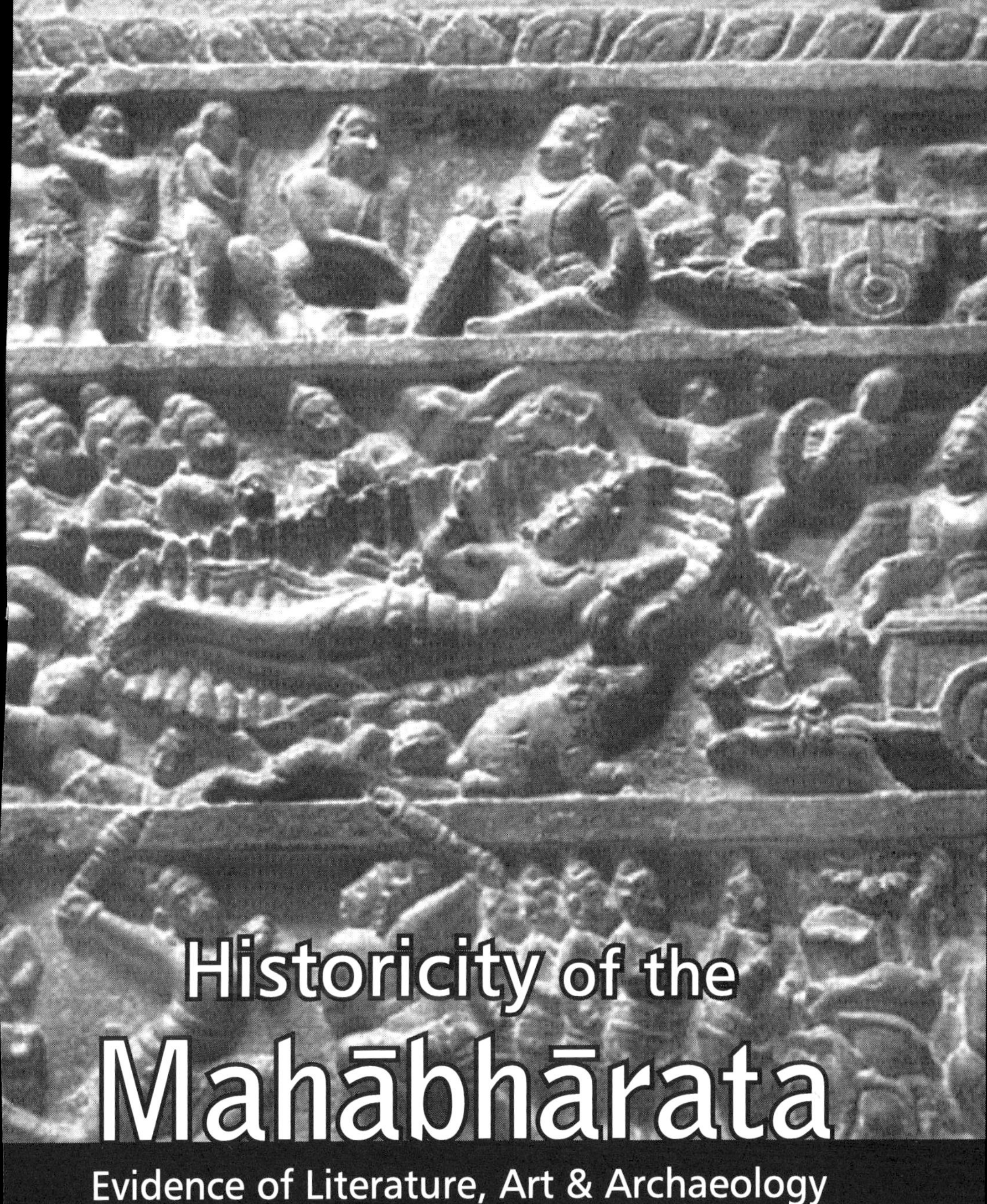

Historicity of the Mahābhārata

Evidence of Literature, Art & Archaeology

Historicity of the Mahābhārata

ISBN: 978-81-7305-458-7

First Published 2013

Published by
Aryan Books International
Pooja Apartments, 4B, Ansari Road, New Delhi-110 002 (India)
Tel.: 23287589, 23255799; Fax: 91-11-23270385
E-mail: aryanbooks@gmail.com
www.aryanbooks.com

Printed in India

Presented to

Sceptics

who are habituated to look at
Ancient Indian Historical Traditions
with ever-suspicious eyes
and dump them as myths

Contents

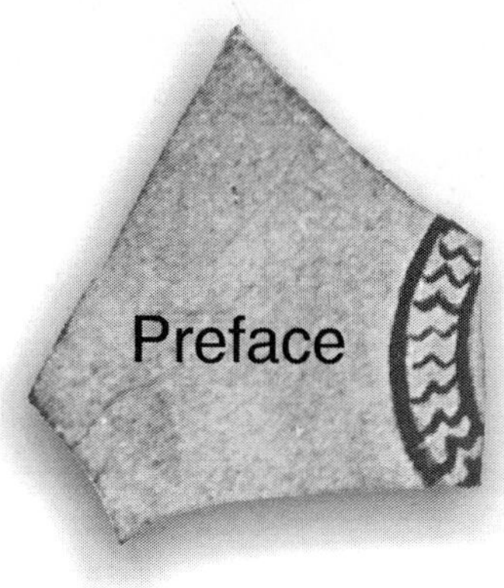

Preface

On April 26-27, 2012, there was an International Conference in Delhi on 'The *Mahābhārata*: Its Historicity, Antiquity, Evolution and Impact on Civilization'. It was organized by Ms. Neera Misra, Chairperson, Draupadi Trust. At it I gave a presentation on 'Historicity of the *Mahābhārata*: What has Archaeology to Say in the Matter?' The presentation appears to have been greatly appreciated by fellow conferees as well as by the audience who agreed with the archaeological evidence that I presented, namely that the epic did have a basis in history and was not the figment of imagination as some people are prone to believe. Further, that the event is likely to have taken place sometime around 900 BCE.

On the evening of April 27, I invited some senior national and international participants to a dinner at my residence. After the dinner was over, there was a further discussion on my presentation during which I answered many a question. Some of the colleagues were aware of the fact that I had published in 1954-55 a full report on my excavations at Hastināpura and a few papers subsequently. All of them, however, suggested that it would benefit the academic community as well as the general reader if I publish a handy book on the subject. The present booklet is in response to this suggestion. May it be hoped that it fulfils the need.

October 2, 2012 **B.B. Lal**

Acknowledgements

In the preparation of this booklet I have received co-operation and assistance from many institutions and individuals. For example, I have used a number of illustrations which had been published by the Archaeological Survey of India, in my Report on the excavations at Hastināpura. The National Museum, New Delhi, has provided me with two coloured photographs. Dr. Nanditha Krishna, Director, C.P. Ramaswami Aiyar Institute of Indological Research, Chennai, has very generously lent me about a dozen photographs, including the ones from Angkor Wat and Bali. Shri S.K. Sharma has helped me in piecing together the illustrations and has also specially prepared some of them for me. Shri Vishnu Kant has assisted me ungrudgingly in collecting various references and has also gone through the proofs and prepared the Index. My son, Rajesh, has gone through the text and has made many valuable suggestions. He has also lent me a hand in going through the proofs. As usual, my wife, Kusum, has been giving the necessary encouragement at all stages. Shri Vikas Arya, the publisher, has been very co-operative all through. To all of them, my grateful thanks are due.

List of Illustrations

The sculpted panel at the beginning of each chapter is from Gupta Temple, Deogarh, circa 500 CE.

Cover: Kṛiṣṇa showing his *viśvarūpa* to Arjuna. A painting from Kashmir, 1850 CE. Courtesy: National Museum, New Delhi.

CHAPTER 1

Introducing the *Mahābhārata* Text

A. INTRODUCTORY

The *Mahābhārata* is the largest of the epics ever composed anywhere in the world. According to the Gita Press, Gorakhpur, Edition (*Ādi Parvan*: 1.81 a and b; 1.101b-102a and 1.102b-103a), it started off with 8,800 verses and was called the *Jaya,** implying thereby that it was primarily concerned with the victory (*Jaya*) of the Pāṇḍavas over the Kauravas. At the next stage, it was called the *Bhārata,* comprising 24,000 verses and, finally, after copious additions, it consisted of 1,00,000 verses and was named the *Mahābhārata*. [*Although the word *Jaya* does not occur in Verse 1.81, it does occur later, in the same *Ādi Parvan,* in Verse 62.20b: *'Jayo nāmetihāso'yaṁ śrotavyo vijigīṣuṇā'*.]

Aṣṭau śloka sahasrāṇi aṣṭau ślokaśatāni ca / 1.81a
aham vedmi Śuko vetti Saṁjayo vetti vā na vā // 1.81b

chaturviṁśatiśāhasrīm chakre bhārata saṁhitām //1.102b
upākhyānairvinā tāvad bhāratam prochyate budhaiḥ /1.103a
idam śatasahasram tu ślokānām puṇyakarmaṇām //1.101b
upākhyānaiḥ saha jñeyamādayam bhāratamuttamam /1.102a

That this caliber of a 1,00,000-verse *Mahābhārata* had been reached by the 6th century of the Common Era is clearly borne out by the Khoh Grant of Mahārājā Śarvanātha, ascribable to 534 CE, which refers to the epic as *Śatasāhasrī Saṁhitā*. It may also be noted that the use of the term *saṁhitā* (compilation) in this inscription and elsewhere clearly shows that the *Mahābhārata*, as it is, may not have been the work of a single individual, but the output of many hands, put together sometime in antiquity itself.

With its 1,00,000 verses the *Mahābhārata* acquired indeed an encyclopedic character. Indian tradition recognises four goals of life, namely *dharma* (socio-religious duties), *artha* (earning of wealth), *kāma* (love and conjugal life) and *mokṣa* (emancipation). The *Ādi Parvan* (cf. below) proudly speaks of the fact that in respect of these topics whatever is there in the *Mahābhārata* is elsewhere and whatever is not in it is nowhere else.

01056033a धर्मे चार्थे च कामे च मोक्षे च भरतर्षभ
01056033c यदिहास्ति तदन्यत्र यन्नेहास्ति न तत्क्वचित्

Such is the all-embracing character of this great Indian saga.

[Note: The Bhandarkar Oriental Research Institute (BORI), Pune, has prepared a Critical Edition (CE) of the *Mahābhārata*, which is in Devanāgarī script. It has been put in an electronic form on the Internet by Professor Muneo Tokunaga of Koyoto University, Japan (revised by Professor John Smith) and is accessible through Google. I have retained the original Devanāgarī version, without converting it into the Roman script. Of the numerals given in the Electronic Version, the first two refer to the *Parvan,* the next three to the *Upaparvan* and the last three to the Verses.]

The *Ādi Parvan* states that it took Kriṣṇadvaipāyana full three years to compose the *Mahābhārata*:

01056032a त्रिभिर्वर्षैः सदोत्थायी कृष्णद्वैपायनो मुनिः
01056032c महाभारतमाख्यानं कृतवानिदमुत्तमम्

He transmitted it to his five disciples who included his son and Vaiśaṁpāyana. They all prepared their own versions (*Saṁhitās*).

01057074a वेदानध्यापयामास महाभारतपञ्चमान्
01057074c सुमन्तुं जैमिनिं पैलं शुकं चैव स्वमात्मजम्
01057075a प्रभुर्वरिष्ठो वरदो वैशंपायनमेव च
01057075c संहितास्तैः पृथक्त्वेन भारतस्य प्रकाशिताः

Vaiśaṁpāyana recited the *Mahābhārata* at the snake-sacrifice (*sarpayajña*) performed by Janamejaya, son of Parīkṣita who ascended the throne after the Mahābhārata War. On this occasion was also present a *sūta* (bard) named Ugraśravas who heard it and later on narrated it at the twelve-year sacrifice performed by sage Śaunaka at Naimiṣāraṇya.

01001001A लोमहर्षणपुत्र उग्रश्रवाः सूतः पौराणिको नैमिषारण्ये शौनकस्य कुलपतेर्द्वादशवार्षिके सत्रे

The *Mahābhārata* consists of eighteen major books called the *Parvans*. These are: 1. *Ādi Parvan* (The Book of the Beginning); 2. *Sabhā Parvan* (The Book of the Assembly Hall); 3. *Āraṇyaka Parvan* (The Book of the Forest); 4.*Virāṭa Parvan* (The Book of Virāṭa); 5. *Udyoga Parvan* (The Book of Effort); 6. *Bhīṣma Parvan* (The Book of Bhīṣma); 7. *Droṇa Parvan* (The Book of Droṇa); 8. *Karṇa Parvan* (The Book of Karṇa); 9. *Śalya Parvan* (The Book of Śalya); 10. *Sauptika Parvan* (The Book of the Sleeping Warriors); 11. *Strī Parvan* (The Book of Women); 12. *Śānti Parvan* (The Book of Peace); 13. *Anuśāsana Parvan* (The Book of Instructions); 14. *Aśvamedhika Parvan* (The Book of Horse Sacrifice); 15. *Āśramavasika Parvan* (The Book of the Hermitage); 16. *Mausala Parvan* (The Book of Clubs); 17. *Mahāprasthānika Parvan* (The Book of the Great Journey); 18. *Svargārohaṇa Parvan* (The Book of the Ascent to Heaven).

Every one of these *Parvans* has *Upaparvans* whose numbers vary, from 3 in the case of *Mahāprasthānika Parvan* (The Book of the Great Journey) to 353 in the case of *Śānti Parvan* (The Book of Peace).

The appeal of and fascination for the *Mahābhārata* became so great that it began to spread out from its 'homeland', the upper

Gaṅgā valley, to regions far and wide. Thus, it travelled to the northernmost region of the subcontinent, namely Kashmir, and to as far south as Tamil Nadu and Kerala. To these Kashmiri, Tamil and Malayalam redactions we shall come later. Meanwhile, it may be added that the echo of the *Mahābhārata* was heard much beyond Bhārata—as far east as Laos. An inscription discovered there, in Tamil Brāhmī characters of the 5th century of the Common Era, refers to Mahārājādhirāja Devānīka and compares him to Arjuna in valour (*Dhanañjaya iva ripugaṇa vijayē*) and to Yudhiṣṭhira in righteousness (*Yudhiṣṭhira iva saddharmī*).

What I have just mentioned shows the influence of the *Mahābhārata* at the elite level. But what is more significant to my mind is its impact on the masses. And here I would like to refer to a real-life fact. It was the year 1988. I was staying in Chandigarh with my son, Rajesh, who was posted there, then a Wing Commander. B.R. Chopra's television serial on the *Mahābhārata* had started screening every Sunday at 9 in the morning. We all were so excited about it that we hurried through our breakfast and sat down in front of the TV well before 9 a.m. Domestic workers and others in the neighbourhood who did not have their own TV set came down to our place and sat with their eyes glued to the TV screen. And this was the case in every house in the vicinity. Reports appeared in the newspapers about this Sunday morning phenomenon, adding that between 9 and 10 a.m. all the streets in the town were deserted—no human beings or vehicles seen.

To revert for a while to the *Mahābhārata* text itself. In its *Bhīṣma Parvan* there occurs the *Bhagvadgītā*, which, to my mind, is the soul of the text. Take it out, and the text remains a mere skeleton—a tale of tales. When on the battlefield of Kurukṣetra Arjuna showed signs of cowardice and his disinclination to fight, Lord Kṛiṣṇa shook him up and told him that it was his duty to fight and defeat the unrighteous Kauravas. He gave a long lecture on *Karmayoga* (Liberation through Action) and stressed—

06024047a कर्मण्येवाधिकारस्ते मा फलेषु कदाचन
06024047c मा कर्मफलहेतुर्भूर्मा ते सङ्गोऽस्त्वकर्मणि

Action is thy duty but reward is not thy concern. Do not hanker after the results, but that does not mean that you should slump into inaction.

Besides the *Karmayoga*, the *Gītā* teaches *Saṅkhyayoga* (Liberation through Knowledge) and *Bhaktiyoga* (Liberation through Devotion). The *Bhagvadgītā* has been translated into most major languages of the world and occupies a very high, if not the highest position amidst the spiritual treatises.

B. THE CRITICAL EDITION OF THE *MAHĀBHĀRATA*

There are two major recensions of the *Mahābhārata*, one northern and the other southern. Within these too, there are many versions. All this made it difficult for an average reader to accept a given version in preference to another. In such a bewildering situation, the Bhandarkar Oriental Research Institute, Poona (Pune), came forward in 1919 with a most laudable plan to bring out a 'Critical Edition' of the *Mahābhārata.* Many distinguished scholars, one after the other, offered their oblations to this *mahāyajña*, including Professors V.S. Sukthankar, S.K. Belvalkar, A.B. Gajendragadkar and P.V. Kane. It took nearly half a century to complete this highly specialised and arduous work.

The first *Parvan*, namely the *Ādi Parvan*, was edited by Professor Sukthankar. In the Prolegomena to it he mentions that about 235 manuscripts of this *Parvan* were known to exist, besides the ones which may have existed but had not come to light till

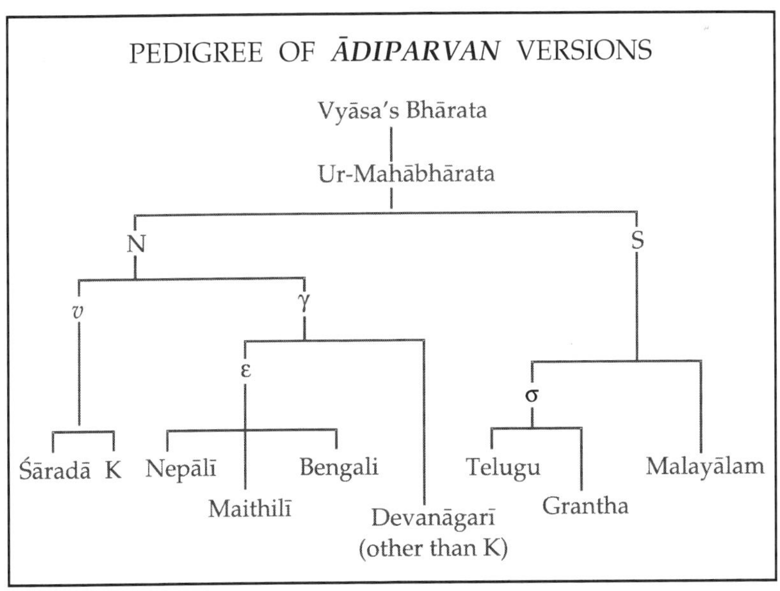

then. Of these, 107 were in Devanāgarī script; 32 in Bengali; 31 in Grantha; 28 in Telugu; 26 in Malayālam; 5 in Nepālī; 3 in Śāradā; 1 in Maithilī; 1 in Kannaḍa; and 1 in Nandīnāgarī. Of these, about 60 were actually utilised in preparing the Critical Edition. Sixteen of these manuscripts bore dates, ranging from 16th–19th century, the oldest being a Nepali manuscript dated 1511 CE.

Incidentally, it may interest the reader that there also exists a Javanese adaptation of the *Mahābhārata*, though only 8 *Parvans* of it have been traced so far. It is ascribable to *c.* 1000 CE. Further, during the reign of Akbar (1556–1605 CE) the great epic was (freely) rendered into Persian, Maulānā 'Abdu'l Qādir Badāyūnī and Shaikh Sultan of Thanesar being amongst the scholars who were associated with this task.

To come back to the Critical Edition (CE). The principle followed in the preparation the Critical Edition was very simple yet very sound. It is known as *brevior lectio praeferenda est,* i.e. the shortest text is to be preferred (as against the longer ones which are likely to be saddled with additions and interpolations). For his *Ādi Parvan,* Sukthankar found a 7984-verse version in the Śāradā script to be the shortest and he placed it at the core. Extra text-material found in other versions was not neglected and was duly incorporated either in the footnotes or in appendices. Thus, the researcher has the full opportunity of looking at the text as a whole.

In an excellent article captioned 'Three Rails of the *Mahābhārata* Text Tradition', published in *Journal of Vaishnava Studies,* Vol. 19, No. 2, Spring 2011, pp.23-69, Professor T.P. Mahadevan analyses the movement of the *Mahābhārata* tradition from the Kuru-Pāñchāla region to Tamil Nadu and thence on to Kerala. He concludes as follows (p. 50):

> We see that by building on the findings of the Poona editors of the CE of the *Mbh,* we are able to place the *Mbh* tradition in a comprehensive perspective, both in time and place. It begins with M_1, the first written *Mbh,* already the complete 18-*parvan* epic, in the Kuru-Pāñcāla country, ca. 3rd–2nd BCE, in a Mauryan Brāhmī script. It arrives in the peninsula on the eve of the Sangam period (50 BCE–300 CE) and functions in the hands of Pūrvaśikhā Brahmans as a template for its self-validating second rail, the M_2 text, plausibly in a proto-Grantha script. At

the Kalabhra Interregnum, M_2 leaves the Tamil country with one Pūrvaśikhā branch, the historical Nambudiri Brahmans, for Malabar to become M_{2m}, the Malayalam version of M_2, in its *ārya eluttu* script. The M_2 text remains behind in the Tamil country with another Pūrvaśikhā branch, the historical Cōliya Brahmans, to become M_{2GT} in the Grantha and Telugu scripts by the Nayaka period (ca. 16th CE) by hosting the NR *a-Mbh*, arriving in the Tamil country with the second Brahman migration, that of the Aparaśikhā Brahmans.

This is a very nice and cosy picture, but, may it be noted that the case for a written manuscript of the 3rd-2nd century BCE is of a circumstantial nature. The argument has been that whereas 'phonology' was the basis for oral transmission of the Vedas, in the case of the *Mahābhārata*, 'semantics' was the basis and, therefore, this text could not go on *ad infinitum* without a written base. Hence, as soon as in the 3rd–2nd century BCE a script became available, the *Mahābhārata* was reduced to writing. Well and good. But what was happening to it before this cut-off date? The simple conclusion is that it was in the hands of bards, all of whom cannot be expected to adhere or stick to one and the same unwritten text. In fact, this bard-to-bard variation is so normal a phenomenon that it can be seen even in some recent cases, for example that of Allahabad Kumbha Mela tragedy of 1954. There exist three versions of this event which differ one from the other in details, though the core story remains the same (see Appendix II). Evidently, therefore, the 3rd-2nd century BCE-text cannot be expected to be the same as was composed by Vyāsa or recited by Vaiśaṁpāyana to Janamejaya. Thus, we are even now far away from the earliest version.

In this context, it may be well worthwhile to quote from Sukthankar's Prolegomena itself (pp. cii-ciii):

> To prevent misconception in the mind of the casual reader, it is best to state at first what the constituted text [the Critical Edition] is *not*. The editor is firmly convinced that the text printed in this edition is *not* anything like the autograph copy of the work of its mythical author, Maharṣi Vyāsa. It is *not*, in any sense, a reconstruction of the Ur-Mahābhārata or of the Ur-Bhārata, that ideal but impossible desideratum. It is also *not* an exact replica of the poem recited by Vaiśaṁpāyana before Janamejaya. It is

further wholly uncertain how close it approaches the text of the poem said to be recited by the Sūta (or Sauti) before Śaunaka or other dwellers of the Naimiṣa forest. [All *italics* are in the original of Sukthankar's own text, since he wanted to emphasize the reality.]

However, all said and done, the Critical Edition of the *Mahābhārata*, published by the Bhandarkar Oriental Research Institute, Pune, remains the best bet at present.

CHAPTER 2

Impact of the *Mahābhārata* on South Indian Literature

As mentioned in the preceding chapter, the colossus of the *Mahābhārata* began moving towards south India around the beginning of the Common Era, through the agency of Brāhmaṇa priests. This process kept on and on as further waves of Brāhmaṇas rolled down to the south. The *Mahābhārata* story, being very powerful and fascinating, began catching the imagination of the local people and the result was original productions in the local languages, based on the archetype, of course with lots of omissions and additions. Besides these regional *Mahābhāratas*, there also began to appear in certain texts eulogies praising local heroes and kings and comparing them, in one way or another, with the Mahābhārata heroes like Arjuna,

Yudhiṣṭhira, etc. The story seems to have gained so much popularity that it began to show off in folklores and folk-dramas. In the following pages we shall deal, though very briefly, with what happened in Tamil Nadu and Karnataka. It is not proposed to deal with other regions of the country since the main focus of this book is on the **historicity** of the *Mahābhārata* and not on its various renderings and adaptations in the entire country.

A. TAMIL NADU

Archaeologically, contacts between the northern and southern regions of India are well established during the reign of the Mauryan king Aśhok (3rd century BCE), since rock edicts engraved at his behest have been found at a number of places in the south. But the contacts are likely to have been much older, since potsherds of a very distinctive ceramic industry, namely the Northern Black Polished Ware (NBPW), have been recovered from a number of sites in the south. In its home region, namely the middle Gaṅgā Valley, the NBPW may well go back to the first quarter of the first millennium BCE and thus its southward movement may be dated to a period around the middle of that millennium. Against this cultural contact between the north and the south, the transmission of some literary texts from the north to south may well go back to the last quarter of the first millennium BCE. With this background, attention may once again be drawn to the paper by T.P. Mahadevan, quoted in Chapter I, wherein he says:

> ... we are able to place the *Mbh* [*Mahābhārata*] tradition in a comprehensive perspective, both in time and place. It begins with M_1, the first written *Mbh*, already the complete 18-*parvan* epic, in the Kuru-Pāñcāla country, ca. 3rd-2nd BCE, in a Mauryan Brāhmī script. It arrives in the peninsula on the eve of the Sangam period (50 BCE-300 CE) and functions in the hands of Pūrvaśikhā Brahmans as a template for its self-validating second rail, the M_2 text, plausibly in a proto-Granth script. ...

In complete consonance with the above-mentioned postulate of a pre-Sangam transmission of the *Mahābhārata* tradition to the south, we do find references to the Mahābhārata heroes

and episodes in Sangam literature. Thus, for example, the *Perumpāṇārruppatai,* while describing the exploits of King Tontaiman Ilantirayan, compares his victory over his enemies with that of the Pāṇḍavas who were only five (*pañcha*) in number but defeated the Kauravas who numbered as many as one hundred. Again, there is an interesting reference in *Chirupāṇārruppatai,* a noteworthy idyll of the Sangam period, to a treatise on cooking by Bhīma, who is known to have acted as a chef in the royal palace of King Virāṭa with whom the Pāṇḍavas stayed incognito during their exile. (See 'Tamil Versions of the Mahābhārata and Studies on the Tamil Versions' by A.A. Manavalan in *Mahābhārata: The End of an Era (Yugānta),* edited by Ajay Mitra Shastri, Indian Institute of Advanced Study, Shimla, 2004)

It is important to note that Pāṇḍya kings set up a Tamil Academy at Madurai. This speaks volumes for the keen interest that these kings took in academic matters. This information is revealed by a copperplate inscription found at Chinnamanur near Madurai. It is ascribable to the 10th century CE. It is under the auspices of this Academy and the patronage of the Pāṇḍya kings that the first translation of the *Mahābhārata* was carried out in Tamil. Although most of the Tamil text is lost, from whatever little is available it is clear that the work was of a high order.

Another work, named *Bhārata Venpā,* was produced between 850–59 CE, under the patronage of the Pallava king Nandivarman III. Although this work too has not been found in full, at least 800 verses are available, covering the span between the *Udyoga Parvan* and the *Droṇa Parvan*. The interesting point about this work is that it is in 'Champu' style. While the verses are in chaste Tamil, the prose part contains a great deal of Sanskrit words. Manavalan, in his paper referred to above, enumerates over ten variations in this Tamil version as compared to the original Sanskrit text. Thus, for example, in the original *Mahābhārata,* Vidura is portrayed as a minister of high ethical calibre and never as a warrior, but in the Tamil version he is depicted as one carrying a bow which he broke as a protest against Duryodhana's unbecoming behaviour. Or, the Tamil version states that Duryodhana's banner had a serpent on it, whereas in the original *Mahābhārata* the banner had an elephant. This change of the emblem on the banner is a feature adopted in other south Indian versions as well. Perhaps in the then prevailing south Indian ethos, the serpent was considered a better signifier of Duryodhana's character than did the elephant!

In the 14th century CE, a distinguished poet named Villiputtūrār produced a version of the *Mahābhārata*, called *Villi Bhāratam* after his name, which turned out to be very popular amongst the various Tamil versions. However, comprising 4,300 verses, it includes only the first ten *Parvan*s, ending with the *rājyābhiṣeka* of Yudhiṣṭhira. This text became very handy for the *pravachanakāraka*s who used it for their discourses, moving from village to village.

The craze for producing fresh Tamil versions of the *Mahābhārata* was so great that even as late as the 19th century CE a poet named Nallappillai came out with his *Bhāratam.* Consisting of 14, 000 verses, it turned out to be more popular amongst the masses than its predecessor, the *Villi Bhāratam*. Anyway, both these versions did the great job of carrying the message of the great Indian epic from door to door in the rural areas of Tamil Nadu.

In addition to producing the full or near-full story of the *Mahābhārata* in the Tamil language, attempts have also been made to write out poems on certain individual episodes from that epic. Thus, we have the *Nalavenpā,* written by Pukalēnti, a 13th-century poet. As the name of the poem shows, it deals with the evergreen story of Nala and Damayantī. Written in the second decade of the 20th century by Subramania Bharati, *Pāñchāli Chapatam* deals with the vow that Pāñchāli took to avenge the insult that she was subjected to at the hands of the Kauravas. Some scholars see in this poem a hidden allegory to Mother India who needed to be delivered from the tyrannical hands of the foreigners.

Earlier we have referred to the fact that the *Mahābhārata* story became very popular in the rural areas of Tamil Nadu. Thus,

there also came into being folk dramas which were staged as street plays along with the *pravachanas*. It has been estimated that there are more than a hundred such plays.

B. KARNATAKA

The other region of south India that I propose to deal with, though rather briefly, is Karnataka. Surprisingly, however, there is no comparison between the two regions. Thus, whereas in Tamil Nadu the *Mahābhārata* story began to catch the attention of the local poets as early as the Sangam Period (early centuries of the Common Era), in Karnataka there was a long wait of many centuries before the first *Mahābhārata*-inspired work appeared on the scene. It was in the 10th century CE that the famous Kannada poet, Pampa, produced his *Vikramārjuna Vijaya* also known as *Pampa Bhārata*, after the name of the poet himself. A little later, but in the same century, another distinguished poet, Ranna, wrote his *Sāhasa-Bhīma-Vijaya.*

In Karnataka, two religio-literary traditions began to emerge, one influenced by Jain religion and the other by Brahmanical. The above-mentioned works of Pampa and Ranna belong to the former tradition. Ascribed to the latter tradition are two important works, namely *Kumāravyāsa-Bhārata* written in the 14th century CE by Nāraṇappa and *Jaimini-Bhārata* by Lakṣmīśa in the 16th century CE. Both these works have become very popular among the masses and are sung even to this day in most of the areas in Karnataka. Besides, folk dramas, based on the *Mahābhārata* stories, have also sprung up and are frequently staged, particularly in rural areas.

Commenting on the significance of the just-referred-to two works, namely *Kumāravyāsa-Bhārata* and *Jaimini-Bhārata*, Shrinivas Ritti, in his paper, 'Mahābhārata in Early Kannada Literature' (cf. Bibliography), says:

> Coming down to the period of Kumāravyāsa and Lakshmīśa from that of Pampa and Ranna, is like entering into the plains after a strenuous, yet enchanting, wandering in the thick woods. The days of the classical *champū* are now replaced by the simpler forms like *Ṣaṭpadī* and the classical old Kannada makes way for

simpler *Naḍu-gannaḍa* or the middle-Kannada, a precursor of modern or *Hosāgannaḍa*. The literature which was essentially meant for learned *paṇḍits* now opens itself up for common people with easy diction. Kumāravyāsa's *Karṇāṭa-Bhārata-kathā-mañjarī* or *Kumāravyāsa-Bhārata* as it is popularly known, and Lakshmīśa's *Jaimini-Bhārata* are the two representative works of this period. The two are the most popular works also, whose recitations are enjoyed and appreciated throughout Karnataka to this day.

CHAPTER 3

Impact of the *Mahābhārata* on Art in India and Abroad

The *Mahābhārata,* though originating in the Kuru-Pāñchāla region of northern India, had its impact on almost all the languages of the country. Likewise, it had also its impact on the sculptural art outside its original area. In fact, this impact extended much beyond India and covered countries like Cambodia, Laos, Sumatra, Java and Bali. Here we shall consider some of the more important presentations in India and these countries. This impact did not remain confined to the past but is a process going on even to this day. What an enduring effect!

It is proposed to select a few important events from the *Mahābhārata* and look for their portrayal in sculptures, in India and abroad.

A. DRAUPADĪ'S *SVAYAṀVARA*

Here are some relevant verses from the *Mahābhārata*. These have been drawn from the electronic version of the epic mounted on the Internet by Professor Muneo Tokunaga of Japan (see p. 2 above). As an explanation of the numbers preceding the text, It may be repeated that the first two digits refer to the number of the *Parvan*. The three digits that follow indicate the number of the *Upaparvan*, and the last three digits stand for the number of the *śloka*. I have retained the text in Devanāgarī script, as given in the electronic version, without attempting to convert it into Roman script.

01176011 द्रुपद उवाच
01176011a इदं सज्यं धनुः कृत्वा सज्येनानेन सायकैः
01176011c अतीत्य लक्ष्यं यो वेद्धा स लब्धा मत्सुतामिति

01176012 वैशंपायन उवाच
01176012a इति स द्रुपदो राजा सर्वतः समघोषयत्
01176012c तच्छ्रुत्वा पार्थिवाः सर्वे समीयुस्तत्र भारत
01176033a निःशब्दे तु कृते तस्मिन्धृष्टद्युम्नो विशां पते
01176033c रङ्गमध्यगतस्तत्र मेघगम्भीरया गिरा
01176033e वाक्यमुच्चैर्जगादेदं श्लक्ष्णमर्थवदुत्तमम्
01176034a इदं धनुर्लक्ष्यमिमे च बाणाः; शृण्वन्तु मे पार्थिवाः सर्व एव
01176034c यन्त्रच्छिद्रेणाभ्यतिक्रम्य लक्ष्यं; समर्पयध्वं खगमैर्दशार्धैः
01176035a एतत्कर्ता कर्म सुदुष्करं यः; कुलेन रूपेण वलेन युक्तः
01176035c तस्याद्य भार्या भगिनी ममेयं; कृष्णा भवित्री न मृषा ब्रवीमि
01179014a एवं तेषां विलपतां विप्राणां विविधा गिरः
01179014c अर्जुनो धनुषोऽभ्याशे तस्थौ गिरिरिवाचलः
01179015a स तद्धनुः परिक्रम्य प्रदक्षिणमथाकरोत्
01179015c प्रणम्य शिरसा हृष्टो जगृहे च परंतपः
01179016a सज्यं च चक्रे निमिषान्तरेण; शरांश्च जग्राह दशार्धसंख्यान्
01179016c विव्याध लक्ष्यं निपपात तच्च; छिद्रेण भूमौ सहसातिविद्धम्
01179017a ततोऽन्तरिक्षे च बभूव नादः; समाजमध्ये च महान्निनादः
01179017c पुष्पाणि दिव्यानि ववर्ष देवः; पार्थस्य मूर्ध्नि द्विषतां निहन्तुः

It is not proposed to give a verbatim English translation of these verses. Only their substance is being given. Thus, King Drupada declared: "Here are the bow and arrows. With these, whosoever shoots down the target shall win the hands of my daughter." On hearing this, most of the kings assembled there, tried their hands but none succeeded. At this, Dhṛiṣṭadyumna, son of Drupada, reiterated the offer, saying that whosoever is able to shoot the target shall have my sister as his wife. Finally, Arjuna stood up to the occasion and pierced the target which fell on the ground. Hailing that achievement, the gods showered flowers on the head of Arjuna.

Fig. 1: Draupadī's *svayaṁvara*: Arjuna shooting arrow. Chennakeśava Temple, Belur, Karnataka. Hoysala, 1117 CE. Courtesy: Dr. Nanditha Krishna.

The accompanying photograph (Fig. 1) shows Arjuna, shooting the target (a fish) without looking at it, but at a dish full of water in which the image of the target was reflected. The picture clearly shows the arrow piercing the eye of the fish which was the target. This scene is depicted on a wall of Chennakesáva Temple, located at Belur, Karnataka. It is in the Hoysala style and ascribable to 1117 CE.

Here is the same theme (Fig. 2), depicted on the walls of Hoysaleśvara Temple at Halebidu, Karnataka. It belongs to the Hoysala Period and is ascribable to 1121 CE. In this picture, however, only the shooter, namely Arjuna, is seen. He points the arrow upwards where the target (not seen) is likely to be.

The *Razmnāmā*, a Persian translation of the *Mahābhārata*, carried out during the regime of Akbar (16th century CE), includes some very good paintings, including one depicting Draupadī's *svayaṁvara* (Fig. 3). In the midst of an assembly of prospective suitors and other noblemen, there stands out a central pole

Fig. 2: Draupadī's *svayaṁvara*: Arjuna shooting arrow. Hoysaleśvara Temple, Halebidu, Karnataka. Hoysala, 1121 CE. Courtesy: Dr. Nanditha Krishna.

slightly bent at the top. At its tip was fixed the target, a fish, which the competitors were required to shoot down. The picture shows Arjuna, with the bow in his right hand. Close by is a hemispherical vessel in which the image of the fish was reflected. The scene is post-shooting and hence there is no fish affixed to the tip of the pole. Instead, the fish lies on the floor pierced by an arrow. A very important part of the depiction is the

Fig. 3: Draupadī's *svayaṁvara*: After Arjuna had shot down the target (the fish lying on the ground), Draupadī garlanded him. A painting from *Razmnāmā*, 16th century CE.

Fig. 4: Draupadī's humiliation: Duśśāsana pulling Draupadī by her hair and trying to unrobe her. Chennakeśava Temple, Belur, Karnataka. Hoysala, 1117 CE. Courtesy: Dr. Nanditha Krishna.

garlanding of Arjuna by Draupadī, which is the culmination of the *svayaṁvara* ceremony.

B. DRAUPADĪ'S HUMILIATION

This is a very crucial part of the *Mahābhārata* story. The Kauravas invited the Pāṇdavas to a game of dice. It was played in a hall at Hastināpura where most of the Kaurava elders had assembled. As actual players, Śakuni, maternal uncle of Duryodhana, represented the Kauravas, while Yudhiṣṭhira, the eldest of the Pāṇḍava brothers, played on their behalf. Śakuni knew all the tricks of the game and kept on winning each throw of the dice. Thus, he first won all the riches of the Pāṇḍavas, then the Pāṇḍava brothers themselves, including Yudhiṣṭhira. Finally, Draupadī was at stake and won by Śakuni. At this the Kauravas greatly rejoiced and Duryodhana ordered Prātikāmin, his charioteer, to go and fetch Draupadī. There was some argument between her and Prātikāmin and the latter came back empty-handed. Greatly annoyed, Duryodhana asked Duśśāsana to do the needful. He went to the room where Draupadī was, pulled her by her hair, tried to unrobe her and dragged her to the assembly hall. This very scene is depicted by a sculpture carved on the walls of Chennakeśava Temple, Belur, Karnataka (Fig. 4).

We have earlier referred to a translation of the *Mahābhārata* into Persian, carried out at the behest of King Akbar (16th century CE). Besides the text, it contains a large number of paintings. Here we reproduce one of these (Fig. 5). It shows, in the upper part, the Kauravas and Pāṇḍavas engaged in the game of *chaupar*, at which the latter lost all their belonging including their wife, Draupadī. In the middle part of the painting she is

Fig. 5: A painting from *Razmnāmā*, 16th cent. CE. In the upper part of the middle register are seen the Kauravas and Pāṇḍavas engaged in the game of *chaupar*. In the lower part of the same register, Duśśāsana is seen disrobing Draupadī (see the enlargement). The register at the bottom shows the five Pāṇḍava brothers, their wife Draupadī and mother Kuntī, all proceeding in an exile.

shown being disrobed by Duśśāsana (see the accompanying enlargement). As a result of their defeat, the Pāṇḍavas had to proceed on a 13-year exile. The lowest register shows the five Pāṇḍava brothers, their wife Draupadī and mother Kuntī marching off through a forest. It may be noted that all of them, except Draupadī, wear dear-skin as their lower garment.

Fig. 6 is an enlargement of the upper part of Fig. 5. In it the game-board is very clear. It is cross-like, each side marked with chequered squares. On the central island (blue in colour) the gamesmen are deposited. One of the persons is throwing the dice. My father, along with his friends, used to play this game and thus I have seen it at close quarters. Made of wood and variously coloured, the gamesmen were plano-convex in shape. The dice, made of ivory, were oblong, with a square section.

Fig. 6: A part of Fig. 5, showing a close-up of the board of *chaupar*.

These were marked with black circlets, their numbers being 1,2,3 and 4 on the respective four sides. It may interest the reader to know that exactly the same type of gamesmen, though in terracotta (Fig. 36), and dice, though made of bone (Fig. 37), have been found in the Painted Grey Ware levels of various sites which, archaeologically, are associated with the *Mahābhārata* story.

Below are given some excerpts from the *Mahābhārata* relating to this episode.

02058031 शकुनिरूवाच

02058031a अस्ति वै ते प्रिया देवी ग्लह एकोऽपराजितः

02058031c पणस्व कृष्णां पाञ्चालीं तयात्मानं पुनर्जय
02058032 युधिष्ठिर उवाच

....

02058037a तयैवंविधया राजन्पाञ्चाल्याहं सुमध्यया
02058037c ग्लहं दीव्यामि चार्वङ्ग्या द्रौपद्या हन्त सौबल

....

02058043a सौबलस्त्वविचार्यैव जितकाशी मदोत्कटः
02058043c जितमित्येव तानक्षान्पुनरेवान्वपद्यत
02060001 वैशंपायन उवाच
02060001a धिगस्तु क्षत्तारमिति ब्रुवाणो; दर्पेण मत्तो धृतराष्ट्रस्य पुत्रः
02060001c अवैक्षत प्रतिकामीं सभाया;मुवाच चैनं परमार्यमध्ये
02060002a त्वं प्रातिकामिन्द्रौपदीमानयस्व; न ते भयं विद्यते पाण्डवेभ्यः

....

02060024c दुःशासनो नाथवतीमनाथव;च्चकर्ष वायुः कदलीमिवार्ताम्
02060025a सा कृष्यमाणा नमिताङ्गयष्टिः; शनैरुवाचाद्य रजस्वलास्मि
02060025c एकं च वासो मम मन्दबुद्धे; सभां नेतुं नार्हसि मामनार्य
02060026a ततोऽब्रवीत्तां प्रसभं निगृह्य; केशेषु कृष्णेषु तदा स कृष्णाम्
02060026c कृष्णं च जिष्णुं च हरिं नरं च; त्राणय विक्रोश नयामि हि त्वाम्
02060027a रजस्वला वा भव याज्ञसेनि; एकाम्बरा वाप्यथ वा विवस्त्रा
02060027c द्यूते जिता चासि कृतासि दासी; दासीषु कामश्च यथोपजोषम्
02060028a प्रकीर्णकेशी पतितार्धवस्त्रा; दुःशासनेन व्यवधूयमाना
02060028c ह्रीमत्यमर्षेण च दह्यमाना; शनैरिदं वाक्यमुवाच कृष्णा

C. THE PĀṆḌAVAS IN EXILE

The entire Draupadī episode upset Dhṛitarāṣṭra who called her by his side, solaced her and finally decided to set her and the Pāṇḍava brothers free. However, before they could reach home, another invitation was extended to them by the Kauravas to come over once again for a bout of dice. This time the condition was that whichever party lost the game shall have to remain in exile for twelve years, and thereafter spend another year incognito. The Pāṇḍavas again lost to crafty Śakuni and they had to remain in exile for thirteen years. (See the bottom register of Fig. 5.)

D. BOTH DURYODHANA AND ARJUNA APPROACH KṚIṢṆA FOR SUPPORT

Apprehending that there could be a war, both Duryodhana and Arjuna went to Dwāraka to elicit the support of Kṛiṣṇa. When they reached there, Kṛiṣṇa was asleep. Since they were close to him, they took the liberty of entering his bedroom. Duryodhana entered first and took a seat near Kṛiṣṇa's head. Arjuna, entering next, stood with folded hands near his feet. When Kṛiṣṇa woke up he saw Arjuna first. He then saw Duryodhana. He asked them both about the purpose of their visit, which they told him. Kṛiṣṇa said that he could offer his army to one of them and himself, without fighting, to the other, and let them choose. While Duryodhana asked for and succeeded in getting the army of Kṛiṣṇa, Ajuna was delighted to have him personally on his side.

Below is given an excerpt from the *Mahābhārata* dealing with this topic.

05007006a ततः शयाने गोविन्दे प्रविवेश सुयोधनः
05007006c उच्छीर्षतश्च कृष्णस्य निषसाद वरासने
05007007a ततः किरीटी तस्यानु प्रविवेश महामनाः
05007007c पश्चार्धे च स कृष्णस्य प्रह्वोऽतिष्ठत्कृताञ्जलिः
05007008a प्रतिबुद्धः स वार्ष्णेयो ददर्शाग्रे किरीटिनम्
05007008c स तयोः स्वागतं कृत्वा यथार्हं प्रतिपूज्य
05007008e तदागमनजं हेतुं पप्रच्छ मधुसूदनः
05007009a ततो दुर्योधनः कृष्णमुवाच प्रहसन्निव
05007009c विग्रहेऽस्मिन्भवान्साह्यं मम दातुमिहार्हति
05007010a समं हि भवतः सख्यं मयि चैवार्जुनेऽपि च
05007010c तथा संबन्धकं तुल्यमस्माकं त्वयि माधव
05007011a अहं चाभिगतः पूर्वं त्वामद्य मधुसूदन
05007011c पूर्वं चाभिगतं सन्तो भजन्ते पूर्वसारिणः
05007012a त्वं च श्रेष्ठतमो लोके सतामद्य जनार्दन
05007012c सततं संमतश्चैव सद्वृत्तमनुपालय
05007013 कृष्ण उवाच
05007013a भवानभिगतः पूर्वमत्र मे नास्ति संशयः
05007013c दृष्टस्तु प्रथमं राजन्मया पार्थो धनंजयः

Fig. 7: Duryodhana (sitting left) and Arjuna (standing right) visit Kṛiṣṇa (lying on bed) for help. Deccan style of painting. Śaka Era 1668 (1746 CE). Courtesy: National Museum, New Delhi.

05007014a तव पूर्वाभिगमनात्पूर्वं चाप्यस्य दर्शनात्
05007014c साहाय्यमुभयोरेव करिष्यामि सुयोधन
05007015a प्रवारणं तु बालानां पूर्वं कार्यमिति श्रुतिः
05007015c तस्मात्प्रवारणं पूर्वमर्हः पार्थो धनंजयः
05007016a मत्संहननतुल्यानां गोपानामर्बुदं महत्
05007016c नारायणा इति ख्याताः सर्वे संग्रामयोधिनः
05007017a ते वा युधि दुराधर्षा भवन्त्वेकस्य सैनिकाः
05007017c अयुध्यमानः संग्रामे न्यस्तशस्त्रोऽहमेकतः
05007018a आभ्यामन्यतरं पार्थ यत्ते हृद्यतरं मतम्
05007018c तद्वृणीतां भवानग्रे प्रवार्यस्त्वं हि धर्मतः
05007019 वैशंपायन उवाच
05007019a एवमुक्तस्तु कृष्णेन कुन्तीपुत्रो धनंजयः
05007019c अयुध्यमानं संग्रामे वरयामास केशवम्
05007020a सहस्राणां सहस्रं तु योधानां प्राप्य भारत
05007020c कृष्णं चापहृतं ज्ञात्वा संप्राप परमां मुदम्
05007021a दुर्योधनस्तु तत्सैन्यं सर्वमादाय पार्थिवः
05007021c ततोऽभ्ययाद्भीमबलो रौहिणेयं महाबलम्
05007022a सर्वं चागमने हेतुं स तस्मै संन्यवेदयत्
05007022c प्रत्युवाच ततः शौरिर्धार्तराष्ट्रमिदं वचः
05007023a विदितं ते नरव्याघ्र सर्वं भवितुमर्हति
05007023c यन्मयोक्तं विराटस्य पुरा वैवाहिके तदा
05007024a निगृह्योक्तो हृषीकेशस्त्वदर्थं कुरुनन्दन
05007024c मया संबन्धकं तुल्यमिति राजन्पुनः पुनः
05007025a न च तद्वाक्यमुक्तं वै केशवः प्रत्यपद्यत
05007025c न चाहमुत्सहे कृष्णं विना स्थातुमजि क्षणम्
05007026a नाहं सहायः प्रार्थानां नापि दुर्योधनस्य वै
05007026c इति मे निश्चिता बुद्धिर्वासुदेवमवेक्ष्य ह
05007027a जातोऽसि भारते वंशे सर्वपार्थिवपूजिते
05007027c गच्छ युध्यस्व धर्मेण क्षात्रेण भरतर्षभ
05007028a इत्येवमुक्तः स तदा परिष्वज्य हलायुधम्
05007028c कृष्णं चापहृतं ज्ञात्वा युद्धान्मेने जितं जयम्
05007029a सोऽभ्ययात्कृतवर्माणं धृतराष्ट्रसुतो नृपः
05007029c कृतवर्मा ददौ तस्य सेनामक्षौहिणीं तदा

Fig. 8: Army of the Pāṇḍavas moving into the battlefield at Kurukṣetra. In low relief, the scene is portrayed on the walls of the famous Angkor Wat Temple in Cambodia. 12th century CE. Courtesy: Dr. Nanditha Krishna.

05007030a स तेन सर्व सैन्येन भीमेन कुरूनन्दनः
05007030c वृतः प्रतिययौ हृष्टः सुहृदः संप्रहर्षयन्
05007031a गते दुर्योधने कृष्णः किरीटिनमथाब्रवीत्
05007031c अयुध्यमानः कां बुद्धिमास्थायाहं त्वया वृतः
05007032 अर्जुन उवाच
05007032a भवान्समर्थस्तान्सर्वान्निहन्तुं नात्र संशयः
05007032c निहन्तुमहमप्येकः समर्थः पुरूषोत्तम
05007033a भवांस्तु कीर्तिमाँल्लोके तद्यशस्त्वां गमिष्यति
05007033c यशसा चाहमप्यर्थी तस्मादसि मया वृतः
05007034a सारथ्यं तु त्वया कार्यमिति मे मानसं सदा
05007034c चिररात्रेप्सितं कामं तद्भवान्कर्तुमर्हति
05007035 वासुदेव उवाच
05007035a उपपन्नमिदं पार्थ यत्स्पर्धेथा मया सह
05007035c सारथ्यं ते करिष्यामि कामः संपद्यतां तव

Fig. 9: Arjuna and his charioteer Kṛiṣṇa on the battlefield. In low relief, the scene is portrayed on the walls of Angkor Wat Temple, Cambodia. 12th century CE. Courtesy: Dr. Nanditha Krishna.

Here we present the photograph of a painting, now lodged in the National Museum, New Delhi, which depicts very vividly the scene of Duryodhana and Arjuna in the bedroom of Kṛiṣṇa (Fig. 7). While Duryodhana sits on a chair near the head of sleeping Kṛiṣṇa, Arjuna, with folded hands, stands near his feet. The painting is in what is known as the Deccan Style and is dated to Śaka Era 1668, i.e. 1746 CE.

E. THE WAR BEGINS

All efforts to settle the issue peacefully broke down and the War began on the field at Kurukṣetra. Massive armies were arrayed on both sides. Fig. 8 shows the the army of the Pāṇḍavas marching to the battlefield. Fig. 9 shows Arjuna on a chariot driven by Kṛiṣṇa. This latter theme is so popular that in Bali we have an excellent modern example of it (Fig. 10). Scenes shown

Fig. 10: Arjuna, with Kṛiṣṇa as his charioteer. Modern; Bali, Indonesia. Courtesy: Dr. Nanditha Krishna.

in Figs. 8 and 9 are engraved on the walls of the famous Angkor Wat temple in Cambodia (Fig. 11). Built by King Sūryavarman II (1112–1152 CE), the temple covers an overall area of about 500 acres. The central shrine, dedicated to Viṣṇu, is enclosed by four successive enclosures, of which the walls of the third enclosure are full of carvings portraying scenes from the *Rāmāyaṇa, Mahābhārata* and *Purāṇas*. The carved panels have been estimated to run up to a length of 700 meters—indeed unparalleled anywhere in the world. See also Fig. 12, a map showing countries of Southeast Asia where *Mahābhārata*-inspired sculptures/carvings have been found.

On seeing the armies and realising that the war would lead to immense destruction, Arjuna told Kṛiṣṇa that he would prefer not to fight:

06023027c तान्समीक्ष्य स कौन्तेयः सर्वान्बन्धूनवस्थितान्
06023028a कृपया परयाविष्टो विषीदन्निदमब्रवीत्
06023028c दृष्ट्वेमान्स्वजनान्कृष्ण युयुत्सून्समवस्थितान्
06023029a सीदन्ति मम गात्राणि मुखं च परिशुष्यति

Fig. 11: General view of the Angkor Wat Temple, Cambodia. 12th century CE. Courtesy: Encarta Encyclopedia, Corbis/Dave G. Houser.

06023029c वेपथुश्च शरीरे मे रामहर्षश्च जायते

06023030c न च शक्नोम्यवस्थातुं भ्रमतीव च मे मनः

06023031a निमित्तानि च पश्यामि विपरीतानि केशव

06023031c न च श्रेयोऽनुपश्यामि हत्वा स्वजनमाहवे

06023032a न काङ्क्षे विजयं कृष्ण न च राज्यं सुखानि च

Finding Arjuna in such a state of mind, Kṛiṣṇa told him not to give up his duty and fight the Kauravas, for they deserved it. This discourse by Lord Kṛiṣṇa, popularly known as the *Bhagvadgītā,* contains the highest philosophy ever delivered to mankind. Its essence is that the soul is immortal and does not die with the death of the body and that one should perform one's duty without hankering after the results. Here are some related excerpts:

06024020a न जायते म्रियते व कदा चि;न्नायं भूत्वा भविता वा न भूयः

06024020c अजो नित्यः शाश्वतोऽयं पुराणो; न हन्यते हन्यमाने शरीरे

06024021a वेदाविनाशिनं नित्यं य एनमजमव्ययम्

06024021c कथं स पुरूषः पार्थ कं घातयति हन्ति कम्

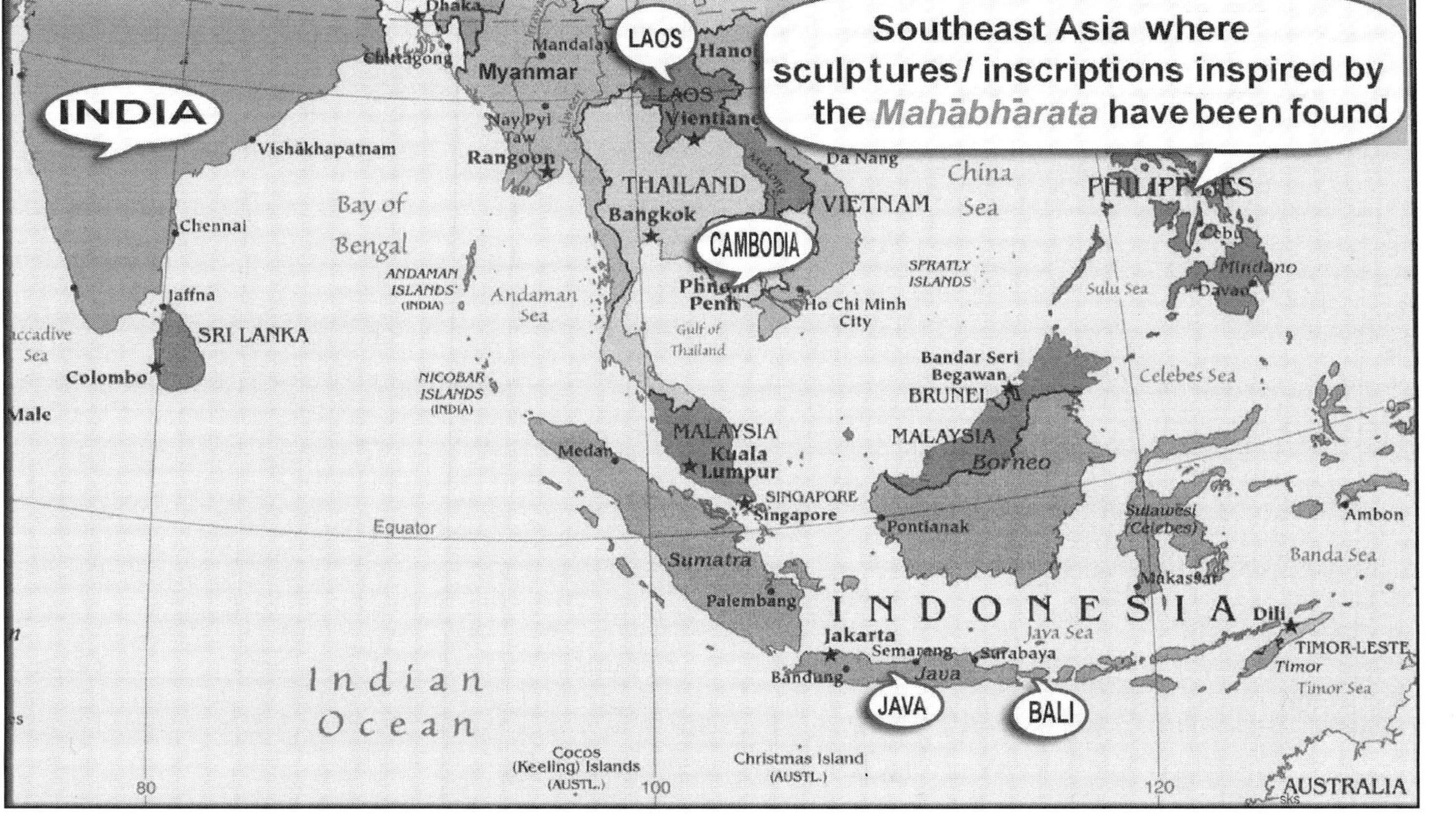

Fig. 12: Map of Southeast Asia, showing countries where Mahābhārata-inspired carvings and inscriptions have been found. Map prepared by Shri S.K. Sharma.

Fig. 13: *Viśvarūpa* of Kṛiṣṇa. Prasat Kravan, Cambodia. 12th cent. CE. Courtesy: Dr. Nanditha Krishna

06024022a वासांसि जीर्णानि यथा विहाय; नवानि गृह्णाति नरोऽपराणि
06024022c तथा शरीराणि विहाय जीर्णा;न्यन्यानि संयाति नवानि देही

....

06024037a हतो वा प्राप्स्यसि स्वर्गं जित्वा वा भोक्ष्यसे महीम्
06024037c तस्मादुत्तिष्ठ कौन्तेय युद्धाय कृतनिश्चयः
06024038a सुखदुःखे समे कृत्वा लाभालाभौ जयाजयौ
06024047a कर्मण्येवाधिकारस्ते मा फलेषु कदाचन

Fig.14: Kṛiṣṇa showing his *viśvarūpa* to Arjuna. In the navel region may be seen Viṣṇu and Lakṣmī (cf. the enlargement). Arki painting, Himachal Pradesh, ca. 18th century CE. Courtesy: Krishna Museum, Kurukshetra.

06024047c मा कर्मफलहेतुर्भूर्मा ते सङ्गोऽस्त्वकर्मणि

06024048a योगस्थः कुरु कर्माणि सङ्गं त्यक्त्वा धनंजय

06024048c सिद्ध्यसिद्ध्योः समो भूत्वा समत्वं योग उच्यते

F. LORD KṚṢṆA'S *VIŚVARŪPA*

Arjuna's delusion was gone and he realised what was to be done. He readied himself for the war. Meanwhile, he requested the Lord to show him His *viśvarūpa* (Universal Form).

06033001 अर्जुन उवाच

06033001a मदनुग्रहाय परमं गुह्यमध्यात्मसंज्ञितम्

06033001c यत्त्वयोक्तं वचस्तेन मोहोऽयं विगतो मम

....

06033003c द्रष्टुमिच्छामि ते रूपमैश्वरं पुरूषोत्तम

06033004a मन्यसे यदि तच्छक्यं मया द्रष्टुमिति प्रभो

06033004c योगेश्वर ततो मे त्वं दर्शयात्मानमव्ययम्

06033005 श्रीभगवानुवाच

06033005a पश्य मे पार्थ रूपाणि शतशोऽथ सहस्रशः

06033005c नानाविधानि दिव्यानि नानावर्णाकृतीनि च

06033006a पश्यादित्यान्वसून्रुद्रानश्विनौ मरूतस्तथा

06033006c बहून्यद्दष्टपूर्वाणि पश्याश्चर्याणि भारत

06033007a इहैकस्थं जगत्कृत्स्नं पश्याद्य सचराचरम्

06033007c मम देहे गुडाकेश यच्चान्यद्द्रष्टुमिच्छसि

06033008a न तु मां शक्यसे द्रष्टुमनेनैव स्वचक्षुषा

06033008c दिव्यं ददामि ते चक्षुः पश्य मे योगमैश्वरम्

06033009 संजय उवाच

06033009a एवमुक्त्वा ततो राजन्महायोगेश्वरो हरिः

06033009c दर्शयामास पार्थाय परमं रूपमैश्वरम्

06033010a अनेकवक्त्रनयनमनेकाद्भुतदर्शनम्

06033010c अनेकदिव्याभरणं दिव्यानेकोद्यतायुधम्

06033011a दिव्यमाल्याम्बरधरं दिव्यगन्धानुलेपनम्

06033011c सर्वाश्चर्यमयं देवमनन्तं विश्वतोमुखम्

06033012a दिवि सूर्यसहस्रस्य भवेद्युगपदुत्थिता

06033012c यदि भाः सद्दशी सा स्याद्भासस्तस्य महात्मनः

Fig. 15: Kṛiṣṇa showing his *viśvarūpa* to Arjuna. A painting from Kashmir, 1850 CE. Courtesy: National Museum, New Delhi.

06033013a तत्रैकस्थं जगत्कृत्स्नं प्रविभक्तमनेकधा
06033013c अपश्यद्देवदेवस्य शरीरे पाण्डवस्तदा
06033014a ततः स विस्मयाविष्टो हृष्टरोमा धनंजयः
06033014c प्रणम्य शिरसा देवं कृताञ्जलिरभाषत
06033015 अर्जुन उवाच

Fig. 16: Close-up of the upper part of Fig. 15, showing Brahmā, Viṣṇu, Maheśa and other deities.

06033015a पश्यामि देवांस्तव देव देहे; सर्वांस्तथा भूतविशेषसंघान्
06033015c ब्रह्माणमीशं कमलासनस्थ; मृर्षीश्च सर्वानुरगांश्च दिव्यान्
06033016a अनेकबाहूदरवक्त्रनेत्रं; पश्यामि त्वा सर्वतोऽनन्तरूपम्
06033016c नान्तं न मध्यं न पुनस्तवादिं; पश्यामि विश्वेश्वर विश्वरूप

We present here three photographs showing the *viśvarūpa* of Lord Kṛiṣṇa. One of these (Fig. 13) is of a carving at Prasat Kravan, Cambodia, assignable to the 12th century CE. It does not, however, duly correspond to the textual description of the *viśvarūpa* given above. Fig. 14 is an Arki painting from Himachal

Fig. 17: Bhīṣma lying on a bed of arrows. Virūpākṣa Temple, Pattadakal, Karnataka, 8th cent. CE. Courtesy: Dr. Nanditha Krishna.

Pradesh, ascribable to 18th centuty CE. It shows the Lord with many heads and arms, each arm holding a different kind of *āyudha*. Various other features are shown all over the body, which include the depiction of Viṣṇu and Lakṣmī around the navel region (see the enlargement). Fig. 15 is a painting from Kashmir, dated 1850 CE, now lodged in the National Museum, New Delhi. Unlike the foregoing example, it shows only one head and four arms. However, in a close-up of the upper part of Fig. 15, we see Brahmā, Viṣṇu, Maheśa and other deities (Fig. 16).

G. BHĪṢMA LIES ON A BED OF ARROWS

This, to my mind, is the most exciting episode of the Mahābhārata War. Hence it needs to be described in some detail. It was the

Fig. 18: Bhīṣma lying on a bed of arrows. Angkor Wat Temple, Cambodia, 12th cent. CE. Courtesy: Dr. Nanditha Krishna.

ninth day of the war. Duryodhana was closeted with Bhīṣma and the latter assured him that he would do all he can to win the war, except that he would not shoot his arrows at Śikhaṇḍin who was born as a woman. A fierce fight ensued between Bhīṣma and the Pāṇḍavas. Bhīṣma's arrows kept on showering at the chariot of Arjuna but the latter's charioteer, Kṛiṣṇa, maneuvred the vehicle successfully towards Bhīṣma. Arjuna knew that the latter would not shoot his arrows at Śikhaṇḍin. Taking undue advantage of it, Arjuna kept Śikhaṇḍin in the front and shot his arrows, one after another, at Bhīṣma. The latter was pierced all over his body with the arrows, fell on the ground and lay on a bed of arrows. Here are some of the relevant verses:

06103097 अर्जुन उवाच
06103097a शिखण्डी निधनं कृष्ण भीष्मस्य भविता ध्रुवम्
06103097c दृष्ट्वैव हि सदा भीष्मः पाञ्चाल्यं विनिवर्तते

Fig. 19: Bhīṣma lying on a bed of arrows. Baphuon, Cambodia, 11th cent. CE. Courtesy: Dr. Nanditha Krishna.

06103098a ते वयं प्रमुखो तस्य स्थापयित्या शिखण्डिनम्
06103098c गाङ्गेयं पातयिष्याम उपायेनेति मे मतिः
06103099a अहमन्यान्महेष्वासान्वारयिष्यामि सायकैः
06103099c शिखण्ड्यपि युधां श्रेष्ठो भीष्ममेवाभियास्यतु
06103100a श्रुतं ते कुरुमुख्यस्य नाहं हन्यां शिखण्डिनम्
06103100c कन्या ह्येषा पुरा जाता पुरुषः समपद्यत

....

06114080a अभिहत्य शरौघैस्तं शतशोऽथ सहस्रशः
06114084a स पपात महाबाहुर्वसुधामनुनादयन्
06114084c इन्द्रध्वज इवोत्सृष्टः केतुः सर्वधनुष्मताम्
06114084e धरणीं नास्पृशच्चापि शरसंघै समाचितः
06114085a शरतल्पे महेष्वासं शयानं पुरूषर्षभम्
06114085c रथात्प्रपतितं चैनं दिव्यो भावः समाविशत्

Fig. 20: Abhimanyu in *chakravyūha*. Rajasthani painting. Courtesy: Krishna Museum, Kurukshetra.

Fig. 21: Janamejaya's *sarpa-yajña* (snake-sacrifice). Painting from *Razmnāmā*. 16th century CE.

Here we give three photographs showing Bhīṣma lying on a bed of arrows. Fig. 17 is from Virūpākṣa Temple, Pattadakal, Karnataka, datable to 8th cent. CE. Figs. 18 and 19 are respectively from Angkor Wat (12th cent. CE) and Baphuon (11th cent. CE), both in Cambodia. All these very graphically depict the event.

H. ABHIMANYU CAUGHT IN THE *CHAKRAVYŪHA*

Another important event of the Mahābhārata War was the entrapping of Abhimanyu, son of Arjuna, in a formation of the Kaurava army, called the *Chakravyūha*. The Krishna Museum, Kurukshetra, has a number of paintings relating to the *Mahābhārata* story. Through the courtesy of the Museum we append here a photograph (Fig. 20) which shows Abhimanyu caught in the *Chakravyūha*. He was finally overpowered by the Kauravas and killed on the battle-field.

I. JANAMEJAYA'S *SARPA-YAJÑA* (SNAKE-SACRIFICE)

At the end of the war, the Pāṇḍavas emerged victorious. Since Abhimanyu had died in the battle, his son, Parīkṣit ascended the throne. He was bitten by a snake and passed away. Thereafter his son, Janamejaya, became the ruler. He wanted to avenge his father's death and put an end to the entire snake community. Hence he performed a *sarpa-yajña* to which hundreds of snakes were attracted and killed by the fire. It is said that only one snake, by name Takṣaka, could survive because of taking refuge under Indra. Fig. 21, taken from the *Razmnāmā,* depicts the entire episode in a vivid manner. In the lower half there is the square-shaped *vedī* with flames of fire into which snakes are falling and getting burnt. Surrounding the *vedī* sit the performers of the sacrifice. In the upper left quarter may be seen a large number of snakes heading towards the sacrificial altar. In the upper right quarter is seen Indra, sitting on a couch with a royal umbrella overhead. Jutting out from his left armpit is the head of a black snake, evidently Takṣaka of the story.

CHAPTER 4

Impact on Coins and Inscriptions

A. COIN OF AGATHOCLES

We shall first deal with the evidence of certain coins since they take us back to a period well before the Common Era. At Ai Khanoum, in Bactria, have been found some silver coins of Agathocles (2nd Century BCE), which bear his name in Greek script on one side and in Brāhmī script on the other (Fig. 22 a and b). On the face bearing the Greek inscription is shown a standing figure of a deity holding a sword (?) in the right hand and a ploughshare in the left, which has rightly been identified as that of Haladhara/Balarāma by Filliozat (*Arts Asiatiques*, Vol. XXXVI, 1973, p. 123). The figure on the other side holds a *śaṅkha* (conch) in the right hand and a *chakra* (wheel) in the left. These are symbols associated with Kṛiṣṇa. All this shows not only the historicity of Balarāma and Kṛiṣṇa, but also the spread of the Bhāgavata cult as far west as northern Afghanistan, something in which the Indo-Greeks too were involved.

Figs. 22 a and b: A silver coin of Agathocles (2nd cent. BCE) from Ai Khanoum, Afghanistan. On one side is portrayed the figure of Haladhara/Balarāma and on the other that of Kṛiṣṇa.

B. HELIODORUS PILLAR INSCRIPTION

Another very interesting piece of evidence regarding the acceptance of the Bhāgavata cult by the Greeks comes from the Heliodorus Pillar Inscription found at Besnagar (Vidisa) in Madhya Pradesh. The pillar, bearing on its top the figure of Garuḍa (vehicle of Viṣṇu), was erected by Heliodorus, a son of Dion and resident of Taxila. He had come, as an ambassador of the Greek king Antialkidas, to the court of Indian king Kāśīputra Bhāgabhadra during the fourteenth year of the latter's reign. This event can safely be placed around the middle of the second century BCE.

There are quite a few inscriptions which refer to the *Mahābhārata* and/or to the principal personalities mentioned therein. However, we shall here limit our choice to about half-a-dozen inscriptions from India and just one from abroad. In India, these inscriptions come from both north and south. However, we shall group them together and try to put them in a chronological order.

C. NASIK INSCRIPTION OF VĀSIṢṬHĪPUTRA PULUMĀVI

Perhaps the earliest known inscription referring to some of the personalities of the great epic is the one discovered at Nasik. It

belongs to the 19th year of the reign of the Sātavāhana king Vāsiṣṭhīputra Pulumāvi (i.e. *c.* 149 CE). In it, his father, Gautamīputra Sātakarṇi, has been compared with **Rāma (Balarāma), Keśava (Kṛiṣṇa), Arjuna and Bhīmasena.** He had effulgence like that of **Janamejaya** (among others). Gautamīputra is estimated to have ruled towards the end of the 1st century CE. (D.C. Sircar, *Select Inscriptions,* Vol. I (1965), pp. 203-07). The following is the relevant quote from the inscription:

.... *Ekakusasa ekadhanudharasa ekasūrasa ekabamhaṇasa* ***Rāma-Kesava-Ajuna-Bhīmasena-tula-parakamasa*** *chhaṇa-dhanusava-samāja-kārakasa* ***Nābhāga-Nahusa-Janamejaya-Sakara-Ya[yā]ti-Rāmābarīsa-sama-tejasa.***

D. KHOH COPPERPLATE GRANT OF MAHĀRĀJĀ ŚARVANĀTHA

K. V. Ramesh ('The Mahābhārata in Inscriptions', in Ajay Mitra Shastri (ed.), 2004: *Mahābhārata: The End of an Era,* pp. 298-313) draws our attention to the Khoh Copperplate Grant of Mahārājā Śarvanātha, ascribable to 534 CE, in which the *Mahābhārata* has been referred to as *Śatasāhasrī-Saṁhitā.* As Ramesh rightly points out, this phrase is of twofold significance. First, it establishes the fact that by the 6th century CE the epic had already acquired the volume of 1,00,000 verses. Secondly, the use of the term *saṁhitā,* which means a 'compilation', clearly shows that the epic was not the work of a single individual, but a compilation of the products of many a hand.

E. SULTANPUR COPPERPLATE INSCRIPTION

From Sultanpur in Rajashahi District has been recovered a copperplate inscription which is dated in Gupta year 120 (= 439 CE). D.C. Sircar (*Select Inscriptions,* Vol. I, pp. 352 ff.) thinks that the plate may have originally been lying at Kalaikuri in the same neighbourhood. Anyway, the important point is that in it there occurs the following imprecatory verse, in which the name of **Yudhiṣṭhira** is mentioned.

Uktañcha Mahābhārate bhagavatā Vyāsena:
svadattām paradattāmbā (ttām vā) yo [*hareta*] *vasundharām (rām)*/
[*sa*] *viṣṭhāyām krimirbhūtvā pi[tṛbhiḥ saha pachyate*] //
....
pūrvva-dattām dvijātibhyo yatnādrakṣya (kṣa) ***Yudhiṣṭhira*** /
mahīmmahimatām śreṣtha dānāchchhreyo-nupālanam //

F. PERJJARANGI GRANT OF GAṄGA RĀJAMALLA I

References to **Abhimanyu** are very rare in epigraphical records. But Ramesh cites (op. cit., p. 304) an interesting example, namely that of the Perjjarangi grant of Gaṅga Rājamalla I, wherein he is praised as follows: ***Abhimanyuriva Subhadrābhinandanaḥ***.

G. A 19TH-CENTURY INSCRIPTION TOO

The lure for equating oneself with the renowned Mahābhārata heroes has been so great amidst the rulers of India that an inscription **as late as 1822** CE describes Vīrarājendra Oḍeyar of Coorg (in south-western India) as ***samasta-praśasta-rājadharmāvadharaṇa-Yudhiṣṭhirar,*** i.e. he was as great as Yudhiṣṭhira in performing the duties of a king (*rājadharma*).

H. AN INSCRIPTION FROM AFAR—LAOS

This practice did not remain confined to the shores of India. Even those Indians who migrated in antiquity and became rulers in parts of South-East Asia, followed this pattern. We cite here an example from **Laos.** It is an inscription running into 64 lines, written on all the four sides of a pillar, at Champassak, a small town in that country. It does not bear a date, but on the basis of the script, which is south Indian Brāhmī, it is assignable to the **5th century** CE. The inscription refers to Mahārājādhirāja Devānīka, whose virtues it extols. He has been **compared with Arjuna in overpowering his enemies (*Dhanañjaya iva ripu-gaṇa-vijaye*) and with Yudhiṣṭhira in righteousness (*Yudhiṣṭhira iva saddharmī*).** [cf. Ramesh, op. cit. pp. 299-300.]

This inscription has something more to tell us. King Devānīka established in his kingdom a holy center, naming it Kurukṣetra, after the *dharmakṣetra* of the same name mentioned in the *Mahābhārata.* **The following verses from the *Āraṇyaka Parvan* of the epic have been bodily lifted and included in the inscription.**

03081173a पृथिव्यां नैमिषं पुण्यमन्तरिक्षे च पुष्करम्
03081173c त्रयाणमपि लोकानां कुरूक्षेत्रं विशिष्यते
03081174a पांसवोऽपि कुरूक्षेत्रे वायुना समुदीरिताः
03081174c अपि दुष्कृतकर्माणं नयन्ति परमां गतिम्
03081175a दक्षिणेन सरस्वत्या उत्तरेण दृषद्वतीम्
03081175c ये वसन्ति कुरूक्षेत्रे ते वसन्ति त्रिविष्टपे
03081176a कुरूक्षेत्रं गमिष्यामि कुरूक्षेत्रे वसाम्यहम्

CHAPTER 5

Problem of the Historicity of the *Mahābhārata*: The 'Why' of the Problem and the 'How' of the Solution

A. THE 'WHY' OF THE PROBLEM

It may be recalled that the *Mahābhārata* calls itself *itihāsa*—a term ordinarily taken to mean 'history'. This is clear from the following two quotations from the *Ādi Parvan* itself.

01001017a **भारतस्येतिहासस्य** पुण्यां ग्रन्थार्थसंयुताम्
01001017c संस्कारोपगतां ब्राह्मीं नानाशास्त्रोपबृंहिताम्
01001024a आचख्युः कवयः केचित्संप्रत्याचक्षते परे
01001024c आख्यास्यन्ति तथैवान्ये **इतिहासमिमं** **भुवि**

But the historicity (*itihāsa*-ness) of the *Mahābhārata* has often been debated. In fact, there exist two extremely divergent views in the matter. To the faithful, everything, major or minor, mentioned in the text is correct to the very letter. For example, he would accept the deployment of **eighteen *akṣauhiṇīs*** in the battlefield, little realising that, according to the laid-down norms, each *akṣauhiṇī* consisted of 21,870 elephants, 21,870 chariots, 65,610 horses and 1,09,350 foot soldiers. Surely, a demographer or a military strategist would doubt the possibility of employing such a large number of men, elephants, horses and chariots. The following excerpt from the *Mahābhārata* gives details of the various units and sub-units comprising an *akṣauhiṇī* and of the overall strength of an *akṣauhiṇī*.

01002013 ऋषय ऊचुः
01002013a अक्षौहिण्य इति प्रोक्तं यत्त्वया सूतनन्दन
01002013c एतदिच्छामहे श्रोतुं सर्वमेव यथातथम्
01002014a अक्षौहिण्याः परीमाणं रथाश्वनरदन्तिनाम्
01002014c यथावच्चैव नो ब्रूहि सर्वं हि विदतं तव
01002015 सूत उवाच
01002015a एको रथो गजश्चैको नराः पञ्च पदातयः
01002015c त्रयश्च तुरगास्तज्ज्ञैः पत्तिरित्यभिधीयते
01002016a पत्तिं तु त्रिगुणामेतामाहुः सेनामुखं बुधाः
01002016c त्रीणि सेनामुखान्येको गुल्म इत्यभिधीयते
01002017a त्रयो गुल्मा गणो नाम वाहिनी तु गणास्त्रयः
01002017c स्मृतास्तिस्रस्तु वाहिन्यः पृतनेति विचक्षणैः
01002018a चमूस्तु पृतनास्तिस्रस्तिस्रश्चम्वस्त्वनीकिनी
01002018c अनीकिनीं दशगुणां प्राहुरक्षौहिणीं बुधाः
01002019a अक्षौहिण्याः प्रसंख्यानं रथानां द्विजसत्तमाः
01002019c संख्यागणिततत्त्वज्ञैः सहकाण्येकविंशतिः
01002020a शतान्युपरि चैवाष्टौ तथा भूयश्च सप्ततिः
01002020c गजानां तु परीमाणमेतदेवात्र निर्दिशेत्
01002021a ज्ञेयं शतसहस्रं तु सहस्राणि तथा नव
01002021c नराणामपि पञ्चाशच्छतानि त्रीणि चानघाः
01002022a पञ्चषष्टिसहस्राणि तथाश्वानां शतानि च

01002022c दशोत्त्राणि षट्प्राहुर्यथावदिह संख्यया
01002023a एतामक्षौहिणीं प्राहुः संख्यातत्त्वविदो जनाः
01002023c यां वः कथितवानस्मि विस्तरेण द्विजोत्तमाः
01002024a एतया संख्यया ह्यासन्कुरूपाण्डवसेनयोः
01002024c अक्षौहिण्यो द्विजश्रेष्ठाः पिण्डेनाष्टादशैव ताः

On the other hand, to the sceptic the epic was nothing more than a mere figment of imagination, there being no basis whatsoever for it. He holds that the text is a motley conglomeration of tales concocted and bundled up together.

Why is there such a diversity of views? To me it springs from the very nature of the text itself. Let us, for the sake of argument, accept that Kṛiṣṇa was a historical figure. The history of northern India is so well known after the Buddha (*c.* 6th–5th century BCE) that there is no scope for placing Kṛiṣṇa after the Budhha. Thus, the former is unlikely to have been later than the 6th century BCE. On the other hand, some of the versions of the *Mahābhārata* include references not only to Yavanas (Ionian Greeks) and Romakas (Romans) but also to the Hūṇas who are known have appeared on the Indian horizon some time in the 4th century CE. Thus, even on this provisional reckoning, there is a gap of more than a thousand years between the Mahābhārata event and the latest version of the text. As mentioned at the beginning of Chapter I, the text started with a meager number of 8,800 verses in the form of the *Jaya*, moved on to 24,000 verses with its name as the *Bhārata* and culminated in the *Mahābhārata* consisting of whopping 1,00,000 verses. All researches to isolate the basic *Jaya* version have so far borne no fruit and there is doubt if this aim will be realised in the foreseeable future. Further, the *Mahābhārata* is indeed not a book on history in the real sense of the term. It is a *prabandha-kāvya* (an epic) and thus its composer had full liberty of letting his imagination fly high. This being so, the text is a colourful blending of facts and fiction and it is next to impossible to isolate the wheat from the chaff.

But then the real question is: Is it all fiction, there being in it no 'history' at all, or is there a basic historical core which kept on being wrapped with layer after layer of fiction?

B. THE 'HOW' OF THE SOLUTION

We shall try to answer the above-mentioned question by examining a variety of evidences: such as that of **non-epic** texts (since the epic itself is the accused) (Chapter 6); and that obtained from the excavations at Hastināpura, the capital of the Kauravas, and excavations/explorations of other sites associated with the *Mahābhārata* story (Chapter 7). These will be followed by Chapter 8, captioned 'Don't throw away the Baby Out with the Bath Water', which will summarise our findings, leaving it to the reader to make up his/her mind.

CHAPTER 6

Historicity of the *Mahābhārata*: Evidence of Non-Epic Texts

A. INTRODUCTORY

Since we are trying to find out if there was any historical basis for the *Mahābhārata,* we would not be justified in using for this purpose the evidence of that very text. The accused, as I said elsewhere, cannot be a witness. The *Purāṇas* too cannot be called to the witness-box, since these belong to a sister family. The witnesses, therefore, have to come from sources other than those of the *Mahābhārata* and the *Purāṇas*. Thus, we shall cite evidence from Vedic literature, viz. the *Atharvaveda Saṁhitā*, the *Aitareya Brāhmaṇa* and the *Bṛihadāraṇyaka Upaniṣad*. This will be re-inforced by the evidence of purely secular texts, namely the *Aṣṭādhyāyī* of Pāṇini and the *Arthaśāstra* of Kauṭilya.

B. THE *ATHARVAVEDA SAṀHITĀ*

We quote below Verses 7-10 of *Sūkta* 127 of *Kāṇḍa* 20 of the *Atharvaveda*. (Edited by Shrirama Sharma Acharya, Shantikunj, Haridwar, U.P.)

Rājño *viśvajanīnasya yo devo-martyāṁ ati /*
Vaiśvānarasya suṣṭutimā sunotā ***Parikṣitaḥ*** *//7//*
Parichchhinnaḥ kṣemamakarot tama āsanamācharan /
kulāyan kriṇvan ***kauravyaḥ*** *patirvadati jāyayā //8//*
katarat ta ā harāṇi dadhi manthām pariśrutam /
jāyāḥ patim vi prichchhati ***rāṣṭre rājñaḥ Parikṣitaḥ****//9//*
abhīvasvaḥ pra jihīte yavaḥ pakvaḥ patho bilam /
janaḥ sa bhadramedhati ***rāṣṭre rājñaḥ Parikṣitaḥ*** *//10//*

I do not propose to give a verbatim translation of these verses. Instead, I would like to highlight the significance of their contents. First of all, may it be observed that three out of the four verses, namely Verses 7, 9 and 10 refer to Parīkṣit and call him a *rajan* (king). In Verse 8, a husband, who is a *kauravyaḥ* (which term might imply that he is an inhabitant of the Kaurava territory), while constructing his house, tells his wife that the king (Parīkṣita) conferred lots of benefits on them. The next Verse (9) states that in the reign of King Parīkṣit, the wife asks her husband whether the latter would like to have curds, buttermilk or some juice. These two verses show that the living conditions were excellent during the reign of King Parīkṣit.

C. THE *AITAREYA BRĀHMAṆA*

Lest it is misunderstood that King Parīkṣit mentioned in the *Atharvaveda* is not the same as the one mentioned in the *Mahābhārata*, we adduce evidence from another Vedic text, namely the *Aitareya Brāhmaṇa*, which clearly shows that the two are indeed the same. The *Aitareya* text concerned reads as follows: (See Sudhakar Malaviya (ed.) 1983, *The Aitareya Brāhmaṇa of Ṛigveda*, Vol. II, p. 1300. Varanasi : Tata Printing Works.)

Etena ha vā Aindreṇa mahābhiṣekeṇa Turaḥ Kāvaṣeyo ***Janamejayam Pārikṣitam abhiṣiṣecha; tasmadu Janamejayaḥ Pārikṣitaḥ***

samantam sarvataḥ pṛithivīm jayan parīyāyāśvena cha medhyeneje

Tura, son of Kavaṣa, anointed **Janamejaya, son of Parīkṣit,** in the style of the great anointing called Aindra (of Indra). As a result of this, **Janamejaya, son of Parīkṣit, gaining victory over the earth, performed the horse-sacrifice.**

This clearly shows the **father-son relationship between Parīkṣit and Janamejaya,** as mentioned in the *Mahābhārata* and the Purāṇas. There are many more references to the same effect in the *Aitareya Brāhmaṇa,* which I am not repeating here. (See Sudhakar Malaviya, op. cit., pp. 1200 and 1222.)

D. THE *BṚIHADĀRAṆYAKA UPANIṢAD*

From this Upaniṣad we get some very interesting information not only about the descendents of Parīkṣit but also about the relative chronological positions of Parīkṣit *vis-à-vis* Janaka, the king of Videha (father of Sītā). The relevant portions of the text are as follows:

Aum. Janako ha Vaideho bahudakṣiṇena yajñeneje; tatra ha Kuru-Pañchālānām brāhmaṇā abhisametā babhūvuḥ; tassa ha Janakasya vaidehasya vijijñāsā babhūva; kaḥ svideṣām brāhmaṇānāmanūchānatama iti; sa ha gavām sahasramavarurodha; daśa daśa pādā ekaikasyāḥ śṛṅgayorābaddhā babhūvuḥ. (III.i.1.)

Oṁ. Janaka, Emperor of Videha, performed a sacrifice in which gifts were freely distributed. Vedic scholars from Kuru and Pañchāla were assembled there. Emperor Janaka of Videha had a desire to know, "Which is the most erudite of these Vedic scholars?" He had a thousand cows confined in a pen, and on the horns of each cow were fixed ten *pāda*s (of gold). (A *pāda* is about one-third of an ounce.) (Translated by Swāmī Mādhavānanda, 4th edn. Advaita Ashrama, Calcutta 1965.)

Atha hainam Bhujyur-Lāhyāyaniḥ paprachchha; Yājñavalkyeti hovācha. Madresu charakāḥ paryavrajām, te patañchalasya kāpyasya gṛihānaima; tasyāsīdduhitā gandharvagṛihītā, tamapṛchchhāma ko-sīti; so-brāvītsudhanvāṅgirasa iti; tam yadā lokānāmantānapṛichchhāma, athainamabrūma, kva Pārikṣitā abhavanniti; kva Pārikṣitā abhavn, sa tvā pṛchchhāmi Yājñavalkya, kva Pārikṣitā abhavanniti **(III.iii.1).**

Then Bhujyu, the grandson of Lahya, asked him. "Yajñavalkya", said he, "we travelled in Madra as students and we came to the house of Patañchala of the line of Kapi. His daughter was possessed by a Gandharva. We asked him, "Who are you?" He said, "I am Sudhanvan of the line of Aṅgirasa." When we asked him about the limits of the world, we said to him, **"Where were the descendants of Parikṣit? And I ask you, Yājñavalkya, where were the descendants of Parīkṣit? (Tell me) where were the descendants of Parīkṣita?"**

Sa hovācha, uvācha vai saḥ, agachchhanvai te tadyatrāśvamedhayājino gachchhantīti; ...... (III. III.2)

Yājñavalkya said, "The Gandharva evidently told you that they went where the performers of horse-sacrifice go. ...."

The above-mentioned dialogue that took place between Bhujyu Lāhyāyani and Yājñavalkya, on the occasion of a sacrifice which Janaka, the king of Videha, had organised, speaks volumes about (i) the fate of the sons of Parīkṣit and, incidentally, (ii) about the relative chronological position between Janaka and Parīkṣit. The story about the sons of Parīkṣit was evidently relatively fresh in the minds of the people. That seems to be the case why the question, namely "Where have the descendants of Parīkṣita gone?" was put by Bhujyu Lāhyāyani to Yājñavalkya. It was evidently not something which Bhujyu had dug up from a hoary past. The reply which Yājñavalkya gave, namely that the sons of Parīkṣit had gone where all other performers of horse-sacrifice go, was perhaps meant, in philosophical terms, to emphasise that performing horse-sacrifice can take one only to a certain point and not to the Ultimate Reality.

The foregoing text also makes it clear that Janaka, king of Videha, was later than Parīkṣit. By how many centuries? It cannot be made out from the above quote. But indirect evidence of other sources, for example, that provided by the names of

the priests contemporary with Janamejaya, son of Parīkṣit, on the one hand, and with Janaka on the other, would appear to indicate that this gap may have been about a couple of centuries or so.

E. PĀṆINI'S *AṢṬĀDHYĀYĪ*

Pāṇini is the most outstanding grammarian of India, perhaps of the world. Although scholars differ about his date, a majority of them are of the view that he lived around 500 BCE. His *Aṣṭādhyāyī* is the most remarkable work on Sanskrit grammar. In it there are hundreds of *sūtra*s dealing with the rules of grammar. These *sūtra*s, incidentally, give a lot of information on a variety of subjects such as geography, social life, economic conditions, etc. In Sūtra IV, 3, 98 there occurs a phrase: ***Vāsudevārjunābhyām vun***. In the interpretation of this Sūtra, there is a debate whether Vāsudeva was worshipped or not (see P. Banerjee, *Early Indian Religions*. Delhi: Vikas Publishing House Pvt. Ltd., 1973, pp. 62 ff.). Be that as it may, it is clear that around 500 BCE the identity of both Vāsudeva (son of Vasudeva, i.e. Kṛiṣṇa) and Arjuna was duly acknowledged. Since these are amongst the primary actors of the *Mahābhārata* story, the historicity of the *Mahābhārata* epic gets *ipso facto* established.

F. KAUṬILYA'S *ARTHAŚĀSTRA*

Kauṭilya, a shrewd statesman, is known to have assisted Chandragupta Maurya in overthrowing the last king of the Nanda Dynasty and may thus be placed towards the end of the 4th century BCE. His book, *Arthaśāstra*, is a masterpiece on statecraft and allied matters. It is a purely secular book without any kind of religious overtones. Its testimony, therefore, is unimpeachable.

The *Arthaśāstra* consists of fifteen *Adhikaraṇa*s (Books) and each *Adhikaraṇa* has a number of *Adhyāya*s (Chapters). The first *Adhikaraṇa*, titled *Vinayādhikārika*, deals with 'Discipline'. Its Sixth *Adhyāya* (Chapter) is captioned *Indriyajaya*, i.e. 'Restraint of the Organs of Sense' with a sub-title 'The Shaking off of the

Aggregate of the Six Enemies'. Since the contents are of immense importance not only from the angle of morality but also from historical point of view, I propose to cite the relevant portions in detail.

Vidyāvinayaheturindriyajayaḥ
kāmakrodhalobhamānamadaharṣatyāgātkāryah //1//

Restraint of the organs of sense, on which success in study and discipline depends, can be enforced by abandoning lust, anger, greed, vanity (*māna*), haughtiness (*mada*) and overjoy (*harṣa*). [Note: The English translation is by R. Shamasastry, Mysore, 1960.]

Karṇatvagakṣijihvāghrāṇendriyāṇām
śabdasparśarūparasagandheṣvavipratipattirindriyajayaḥ //2//

Absence of discrepancy (*avipratipatti*) in the perception of sound, touch, colour, flavour and scent by means of the ear, the skin, the eyes, the tongue and the nose is what is meant by the restraint of the organs of sense.

Śāstrārthānuṣṭhānam vā //3//
kṛitsnam hi śāstramidamindriyajayaḥ //4//

Strict observance of precepts of sciences also means the same, for the sole aim of all the sciences is nothing but restraint of the organs of sense.

tadviruddhavṛittivaśyendriyaśchāturantopi rājā sadyo vinaśyati //5//

Whosoever is of reverse character, whoever has not his organs of sense under his control, will soon perish, though possessed of the whole earth bounded by the four quarters.

Yathā Dāṇdakyo nāma bhojaḥ kāmadbrāhmaṇa-
kanyāmabhimanyamānaḥ sabandurāsṭro vinanāśa //6//

For example, Bhoja known also by the name Dāṇḍakya, making a lascivious attempt on a Brāhmaṇa maiden, perished along with his kingdom and relations.

Karālaścha Vaidehaḥ //7//

So also Karāla, the Vaideha.

Kopāj Janamejayo brāhmaṇeṣu *Vikrāntas Tāljaṅghascha Bhṛiguṣu //8//*

Likewise Janamejaya, under the influence of anger against Brāhmans, *as well as Tālajaṅgha* ***against*** *the family of the Bhṛigus.*

Lobhādailaśchāturvarṇyamatyāhārayamāṇaḥ
sauvīraśchājabinduḥ //9//

Aila in his attempt under the influence of greed to make exactions from Brāhmans, as well as Ajabindu, the Sauvīra (in a similar attempt).

Mānād ***Rāvaṇaḥ*** *paradārānaprayachchhan //10//*

Rāvaṇa, unwilling under the influence of vanity to restore a stranger's wife.

Duryodhano *rājyādaṁśam cha //11//*

As well as **Duryodhana** to part with a portion of his kingdom.

To begin with, the text enjoins that one must abstain from *kāma* (lust), *krodha* (anger), *lobha* (greed), *māna* (vanity), *mada* (haughtiness), and *harṣa* (overjoy) and then warns that by not following these guidelines one is liable to run into great difficulties. This general postulation is followed by specific instances of well-known individuals, mostly kings, who had to face disastrous consequences because they violated one or the other of the preceding injunctions.

Though other names are also mentioned in the list of sufferers from the severe consequences, I will draw attention to the names of **Janamejaya, Rāvaṇa** and **Duryodhana** who are of importance in our present historical query.

Janamejaya is stated to have suffered heavily because of his angry behaviour against Brāhmans. This misfortune of Janamejaya has been referred to in many other texts, including the *Matsya Purāṇa*. That this Janamejaya was none other than the son of Parīkṣit is also clear from a number of other references, for example, in the *Aitareya Brāhmaṇa*.

The last line quoted above from the *Arthaśāstra* refers to **Duryodhana** who, because of his vanity, refused to part even with a small portion of his kingdom. It may be recalled that the Pāṇḍavas had offered that if the Kauravas gave them just five villages the war could be avoided, but the latter refused to accept the request.

The foregoing references to **Janamejaya** and **Duryodhana** in a purely secular text are proofs of their historicity; and since these are eminent personages in the *Mahābhārata* story, its historicity gets *ipso facto* established.

(Incidentally, the reference in the *Arthaśāstra* to Rāvaṇa who too, under the influence of vanity, was unwilling to restore a stranger's wife [Sītā] is an independent proof the historicity of the *Rāmāyaṇa* as well.)

CHAPTER 7

Evidence of Excavations and Explorations at the Mahābhārata Sites

A. COMPLICATED NATURE OF THE PROBLEM

At the cost of repetition, I would like to recall what has already been stated at the beginning of Chapter 5. Briefly, it is as follows. There are two extremely divergent views about the historicity of the *Mahābhārata*. To the faithful, every event, major or minor, and every description, howsoever unusual, is true to the very letter: be it the deployment of millions of soldiers in the battlefield at Kurukṣetra at the time of the Mahābhārata War. The firm believer in the authenticity of these epics would care less if a demographer or military strategist doubted the deployment of a number of *akṣauhiṇī* units in the Mahābhārata War, even though each *akṣauhiṇī* unit, according to the laid-down norms, comprised 21,870 elephants, 21,870 chariots, 65,610 horses

and 1,09,350 footsoldiers. On the other hand, to a complete non-believer in ancient Indian tradition, these epics are nothing more than mere figments of imagination. He holds that the *Mahābhārata* is nothing more than a conglomeration of a series of tales written from time to time to suit certain situations.

B. AN ARCHAEOLOGIST FACES THE CHALLENGE

What does an archaeologist do to face such a challenge? His approach, as usual, is earthly, down to earth. Thus, as an archaeologist I thought that the best way, and evidently the only way open to an archaeologist, was to explore and excavate the various sites associated with the Mahābhārata story and to find out if these could throw any light on the issue. In this context, a very encouraging factor was that **all the sites associated with the Mahābhārata story continue to bear the same name even to this day.** For example, there is only one Hastināpura, one Mathurā, one Kurukṣetra and so on. Thus, there is no confusion on that account and one can confidently treat the basic archaeological data recovered from these sites as authentic (see Fig. 23).

Before going deep into the archaeological evidence, it may be worthwhile to narrate in a nutshell the main part of the Mahābhārata story in order to let the unfamiliar reader know which sites were associated with that story and in what manner. The key-site in the story is, of course, Hastināpura which was the capital of the Kauravas. Going by the same name even to this day, it is situated on the right bank of the Gaṅgā in Meerut District of Uttar Pradesh (cf. Fig. 23). (Incidentally, in the *Ādi Parvan* of the *Mahābhārata* it is mentioned as Hāstinapura from which the present name is evidently derived.) As is well known, there was a dispute between the Kauravas and their cousins, the Pāṇḍavas, over the throne. The Kauravas held the reins, but the Pāṇḍavas contested the same. Driven by this enmity, the former thought of eliminating the latter by burning them alive in a lac-house (*lākṣāgṛiha*) which they got specially built for the purpose at a place called Vāraṇāvata (modern Barnava), located at the junction of the Kṛiṣṇī and Hindon rivers, again in the same Meerut District. The Pāṇḍavas got a scent of the plot and managed to escape before its execution. They traveled westwards and lived in a forest. Meanwhile, they learnt about

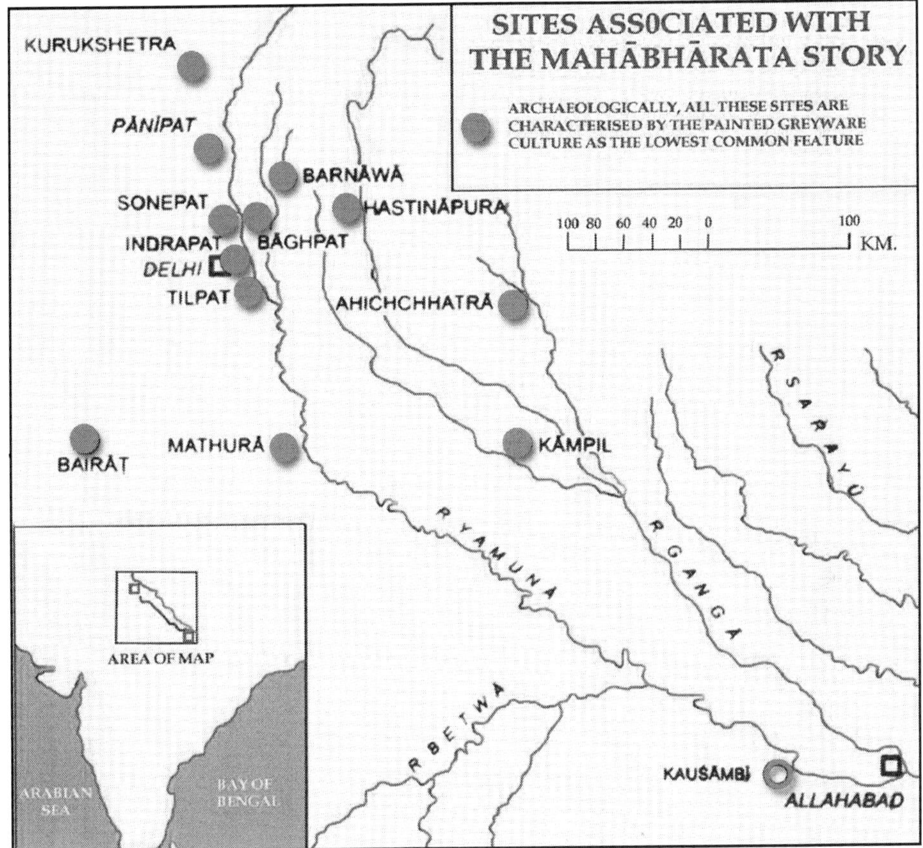

Fig. 23: Sites associated with the Mahābhārata story.

the *svayaṁvara* of Draupadī and went to Kāmpilya, the capital of the southern Pañchāla region. There, Arjuna succeeded in shooting the assigned target and won the hands of Draupadī. Today this place is known as Kampil, which is clearly a derivative from the ancient name. It is located in Farrukhabad District of Uttar Pradesh. As the story develops, the Pāṇḍavas lost their all to the Kauravas at a game of dice and were forced to stay in exile for a total period of thirteen years. During the course of the exile they reached a place called Virāṭanagara which is the same as modern Bairat in District Jaipur, Rajasthan. The then local king, Virāṭa, after whom the place was named, welcomed the Pāṇḍavas and provided them all possible facilities. Having lived at Virāṭanagara for a pretty long time, the Pāṇḍavas sent a message to the Kauravas that the former would not lay their claim to the throne if they were given just five villages. There is some discrepancy between the literary evidence and local tradition about the exact names of these five villages. However, these are generally believed to have been, from north to south, as follows: Pāṇiprastha (modern Panipat) and Śoṇaprastha (modern Sonipat), both in Haryana, Vṛikaprastha (modern Baghpat) in Uttar Pradesh, Indraprastha (Puranā Qila area in Delhi) and Tilaprastha (modern Tilpat), again in Haryana. Prima facie this demand appears to be innocuous, but there was indeed more to it than meets the eye. Had the Kauravas agreed to surrender these five villages to the Pāṇḍavas, the latter would have got full control of the Yamunā system over a long stretch, from Panipat in the north to Tilpat in the south. On the east of the Gaṅgā, the Pāṇḍavas already had their allies, viz. the Pañchālas, whose daughter, Draupadī, was married to them. (The Pañchālas ruled from two places, namely Ahichchhatrā in Bareilly District and Kāmpilya in Farrukhabad District, both in Uttar Pradesh.) Thus, had the Kauravas made over those five villages to the Pāṇḍavas, the former would have been completely sandwiched. Fully realising the implications of this request of the Pāṇḍavas, the Kauravas turned it down. The ultimate result was the Mahābhārata War, which was fought at Kurukṣetra, a place in Haryana that continues to be called by the same name even today. Lord Kṛiṣṇa, who sided with the Pāṇḍavas, was born at Mathurā, a place going by that very name in Uttar Pradesh.

Of the sites mentioned above, Hastināpura, Indraprastha, Tilprastha, Mathurā, Ahichchhatrā and Kāmpilya have been excavated and the rest subjected to thorough exploration. Since Hastināpura is the key-site in the story, the results of the excavations carried out there are given in some detail below.

C. EXCAVATIONS AT HASTINĀPURA, 1950–52

Excavations at Hastināpura were carried out by the present writer way back in 1950–52 (Lal 1954–55). As already mentioned, the site is located on the right bank of the Gaṅgā, in Meerut District of Uttar Pradesh. Though the main stream now flows a few kilometers away on the east, there does exist a minor channel not far from the site and is known as the Būḍhī Gaṅgā, i.e. Old Gaṅgā, implying that it was here that the river used to flow in antiquity. The ancient mound stretches along the river for a

Fig. 24: Hastināpura: A view of the ancient mound, showing Trench HST-1 which was laid right across it. Courtesy: Archaeological Survey of India (ASI).

little less than a kilometer and rises at places to a height of about 18 meters above the surrounding ground level. Widthwise, it measures only one-fourth of a kilometer, but this does not represent the original width of the settlement since, as would be shown later, a good bit of the riverside part of the mound had been washed away by a mighty flood in the river in ancient times.

Though the site was not subjected to large-scale horizontal excavations, quite a few trenches were laid out at different parts of the mound in order to ensure that a complete stratigraphic sequence was obtained. In fact, one of the trenches, named HST-1, was laid right across the mound to get a running story from one end to the other (Fig. 24). Vertically, five periods of occupation were identified, with a break between them all (Fig. 25). The characteristic features of these periods, from bottom upwards, were as follows.

The natural soil consisted of a series of layers of clay and sand over which lay the remains of Period I. It was distinguished

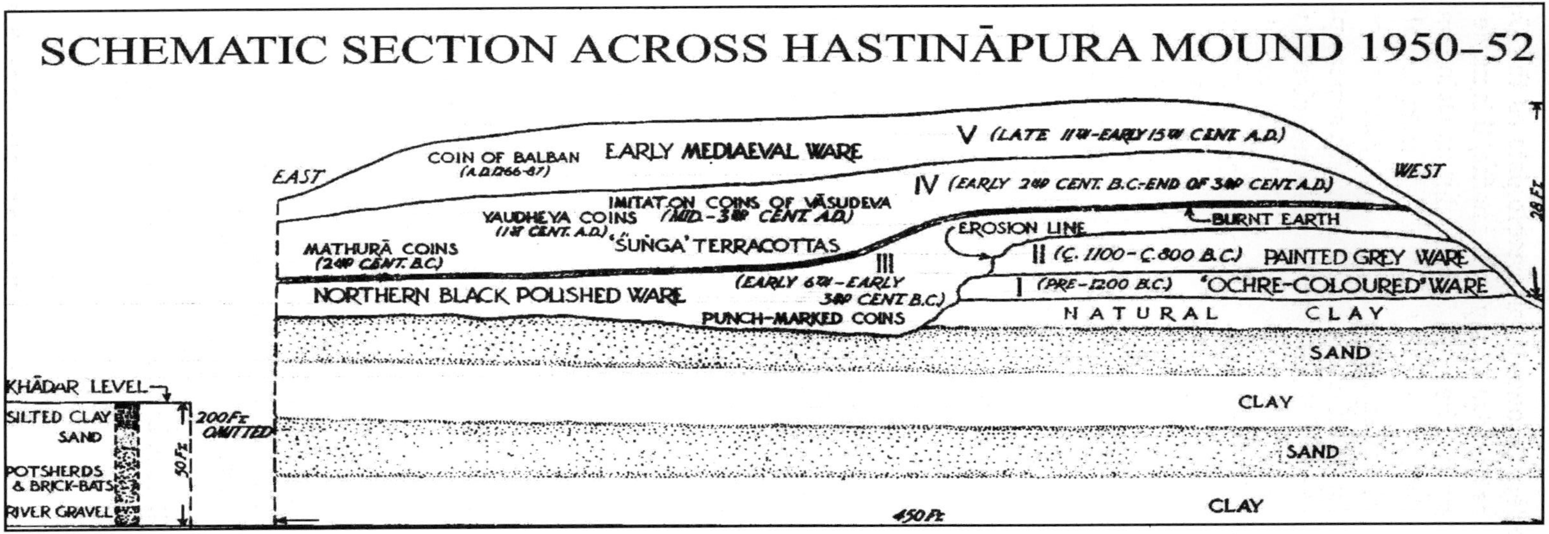

Fig. 25: Hastināpura: Schematic Section right across the mound, 1950–52. Courtesy: ASI.

by a kind of pottery known to archaeologists as the Ochre Colour Ware. In the absence of any better name, this name was given to the pottery just because it left ochrous stains on the fingers when handled. No complete specimens were found and only small fragments lay embedded sporadically in a deposit of yellowish-brown clay, 30-40 cm in thickness, which imperceptibly merged into the natural soil underneath. No other objects were met with. However, evidence from other Ochre Colour Ware sites indicates that this ware often bore a red slip and was also sometimes painted with designs in black colour. The evidence from a site named Saipai, in District Etawah, Uttar Pradesh, conclusively shows that this ware was associated with what are known as the Copper Hoards. Besides other simpler types of tools, these Hoards include harpoons, antennae swords, spearheads and anthropomorphic figures. However, as already stated, no such tool or, for that matter, any other antiquity was met with in the Ochre Colour Ware deposit at Hastināpura.

In this context it may be added that recently (2004–06) a site called Sanauli, in District Baghpat of Uttar Pradesh, was excavated by Dr. D.V. Sharma of the Archaeological Survey of India. Over here a number of human graves were discovered, in one of which a typical antennae sword was also found (*Puratattva*, Vol. 36, 2006, pp. 166 ff.). The accompanying pottery was a red ware, sometimes slipped and painted with designs in black color. There is a possibility that this pottery may have had some relationship with late Haṛappan ware, though the same remains to be duly established.

To return to Hastināpura. After an interval of time, the duration of which it is difficult to determine but may have been anything up to half a millennium, the site was again occupied. This time by the people who used a very distinctive pottery called the Painted Grey Ware. As the name indicates, it was a ware with grey surface (and also a grey core), which was the result of its having been fired under reducing conditions in the kiln. On the surface, both inside and outside, there were designs painted in black color, which included, besides simple horizontal or oblique lines, swastikas, sigmas, chains of short spirals, concentric circles, etc.(Fig.26). The more noteworthy shapes in this ware were dishes, bowls and globular drinking vessels (Figs. 27, 28 and 29). Though the associated culture-complex

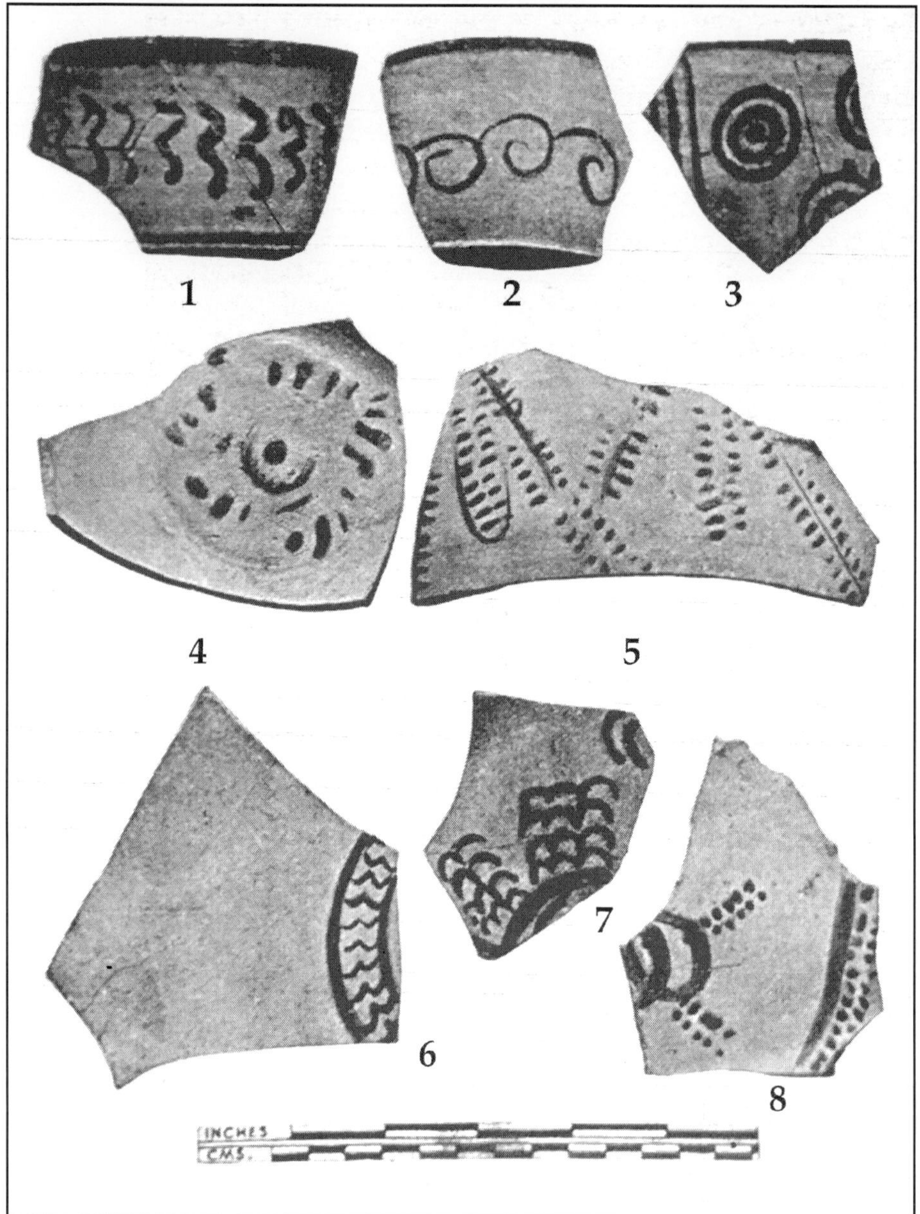

Fig. 26: Painted Grey Ware: 1, 2 and 6 from Ahichchhatrā; the rest from Panipat. Courtesy: ASI.

has since come to be known after this particular kind of pottery, as the Painted Grey Ware Culture, the fact remains that this pottery was the de luxe ware and accounted for only 10 to 15 percent of the total pottery. There were also some specimens of a

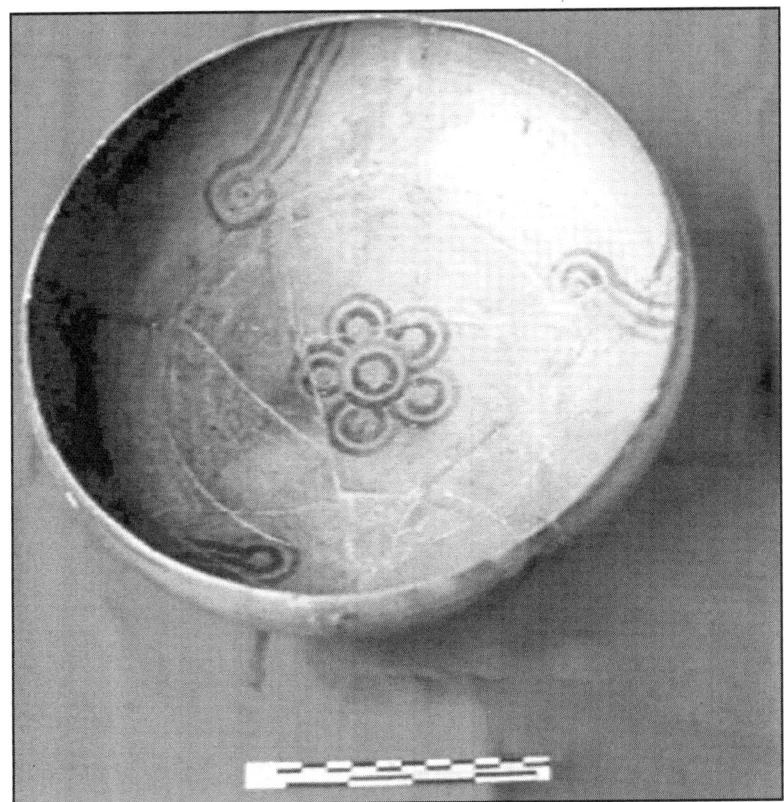

Fig. 27: A dish of Painted Grey Ware.

black-slipped ware, but the majority was that of a red ware, sometimes slipped.

As already mentioned, the excavations were not horizontal in nature. Hence no large-scale plans of houses were encountered. However, walls of mud or mudbricks were duly met with, so also a few examples of kiln-fired bricks. In order to give a better idea of the Painted Grey Ware Culture as a whole, we include here the data from other excavated sites of this culture-complex. Thus, the evidence from Bhagwanpura would indicate that some of the houses could have as many as thirteen rooms, besides a large open courtyard (Fig. 30; Joshi 1993). Bhagwanpura has also yielded evidence of substantial use of kiln-fired bricks.

In so far as the use of metal is concerned, it appears that there were two stages in the life of the Painted Grey Ware, in the earlier of which only copper/bronze was used, but in the

Fig. 28: A bowl of Painted Grey Ware.

later it was iron as well. Whereas some of the PGW sites in Panjab and Haryana belonged to the former stage, most of the sites in Uttar Pradesh have shown use of iron. The combined evidence from Hastināpura itself and from a site called Atranjikhera in District Aligarh, Uttar Pradesh (Gaur 1983) indicates that the iron objects included tools for domestic use such as nails, hooks, axes and tongs and those that may have been used in warfare such as arrowheads, spearheads and daggers (Fig. 31). Jodhpura in Rajasthan has yielded evidence of a furnace with a side-hole into which the nozzle of the bellows could have been inserted to pump in air to raise the level of the heat as necessary. The use of iron by the Painted Grey Ware people is in marked contrast to its total absence during the Haṛappan times. Another noteworthy technological aspect of

Fig. 29: A 'dining set' of Painted Grey Ware, showing a dish (*thālī*), one large and two small bowls (*kaṭorīs*) and a drinking vessel (*loṭā*), put together from different Mahābhārata sites.

the PGW Culture was the manufacture of a variety of glass objects.

Agriculture and cattle-breeding seem to have been the mainstay of these people. The principal crops cultivated by them

Fig. 30: A house consisting of thirteen rooms and a courtyard discovered in the Painted Grey Ware levels at Bhagwanpura. Courtesy: ASI.

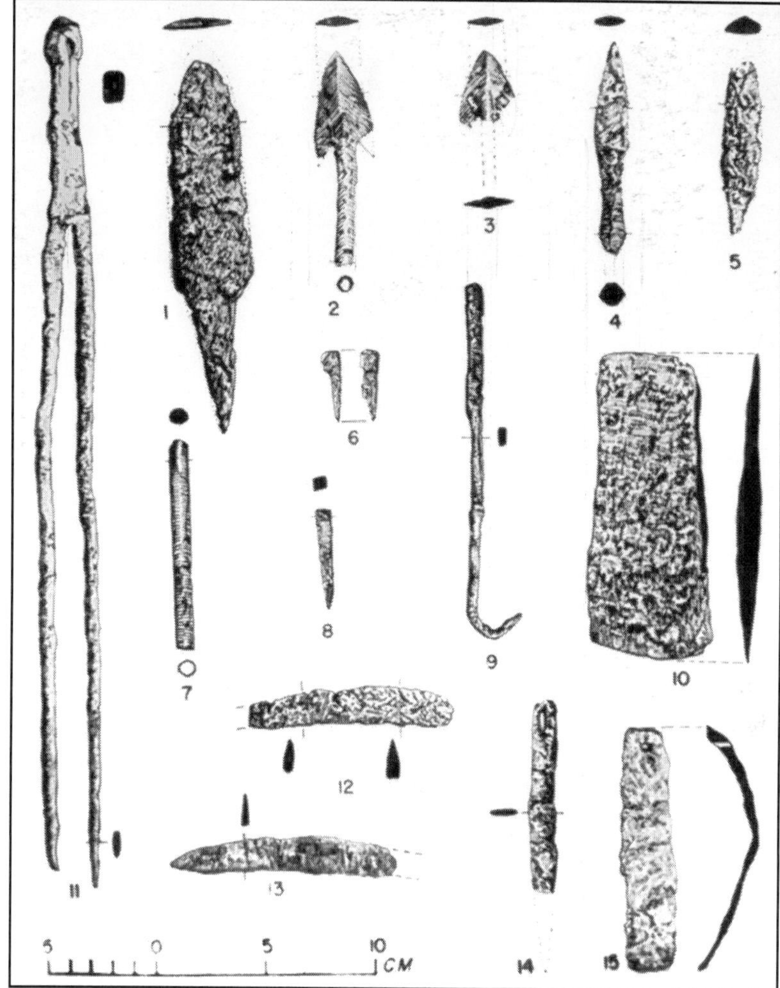

Fig. 31: Iron objects from different sites, associated with the Painted Grey Ware Culture.

were those of wheat, barley and rice. The domesticated animals included the cattle, buffalos, sheep, pigs and last but not least the horse. Wild animals were also hunted for meat and so also fishing was done.

The small finds associated with the Painted Grey Ware Culture included stone-moulds for jewellery (Fig. 32), beads of semi-precious stones, antimony rods and nail-cutters of copper (Fig. 33), ivory combs, earstuds, mirror handles and barbed arrowheads of bone (Fig. 34). Amongst the terracotta figurines

Fig. 32: Stone-mould for casting jewellery, associated with the Painted Grey Ware Culture.

special mention may be made of those having a fiddle-shaped body with pinpoint decoration. This type continued well into the subsequent Northern Black Polished Ware Period and had a very wide distribution in terms of space. Of particular interest was a potsherd on which were engraved intersecting circles with centres duly marked (Fig. 35). This not only shows the knowledge of geometry but also suggests the existence of a divider-like instrument.

Amongst the games played by the Painted Grey Ware people that of *chaupaṛ* or *chausar* deserves special mention. The game continues even to this day. The board is usually made of cloth and has the form of a cross with all the four arms being of equal size. On each arm there are three rows of squares. The gamesmen, coloured and usually made of wood, are plano-convex in shape, while the dice are square-sectioned oblong pieces, generally of ivory and marked on respective sides with blind holes numbering 1, 2, 3 and 4. It is obvious that one cannot expect the survival of a cloth-made board of the PGW times, because of the hot and humid climate of our country. However, the

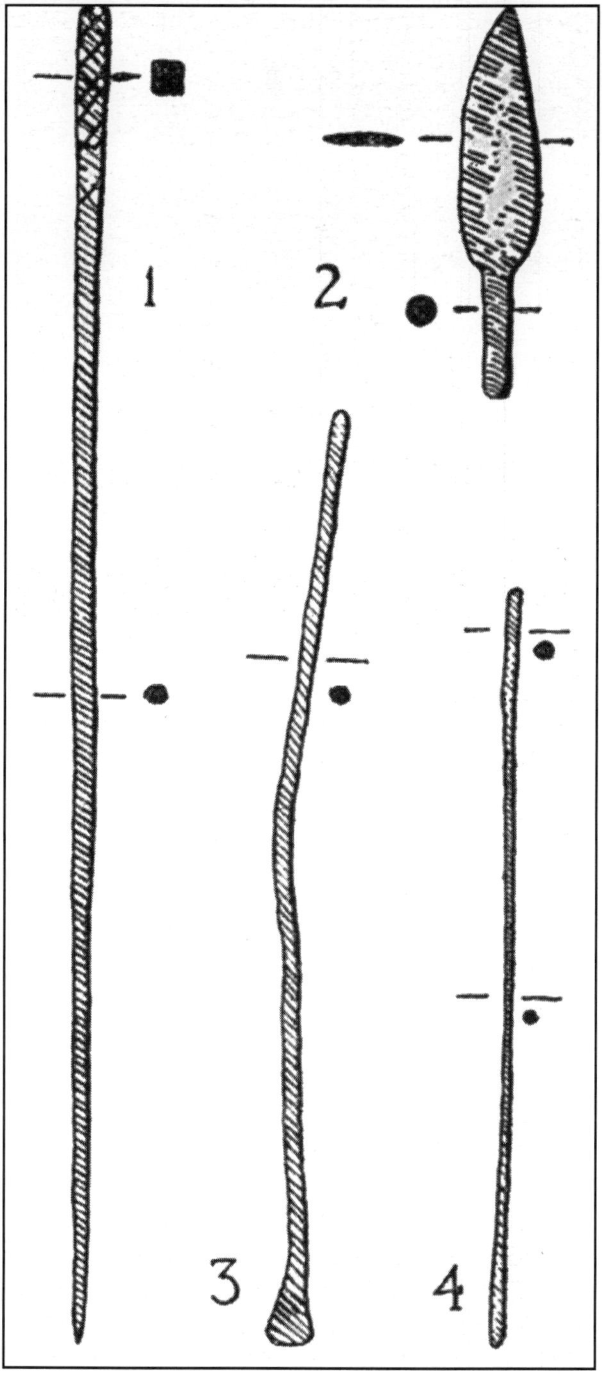

Fig. 33: Copper objects from the Painted Grey Ware levels of Hastināpura. Courtesy: ASI.

Fig. 34: Bones and ivory objects associated with the Painted Grey Ware Culture.

excavations at various sites have duly yielded gamesmen of the aforesaid shape, though in terracotta (Fig. 36), and dice, usually made of bone and bearing the aforementioned kind of the numbering arrangement, i. e. 1,2,3 and 4 (Fig. 37). In this context, it may incidentally be mentioned that it was at this game that the Kauravas defeated the Pāṇḍavas. (See above, p. 20 and Figs. 5 and 6).

The Painted Grey Ware occupation at Hastināpura continued for quite some time, accounting for a thickness of about 2.5 meters. However, its end was sudden and sad. An enormous flood of the Gaṅgā washed away a considerable portion of the settlement on the riverfront, with the result that the site had to be abandoned. The evidence of this flood and of the severe damage it inflicted was duly discovered in the excavation. A huge scar left by the erosion was noted on the eastern face of the mound (Fig. 38). At the foot of this erosional scar, there lay scattered a part of the washed-away material, overlain by layers of silt and sand (Fig. 39). On finding this kind of evidence in the

Fig. 35: A potsherd with intersecting circles incised on it. Associated with the Painted Grey Ware Culture.

excavation, it just occurred to us that it was not unlikely that some of the washed-away material may still be lying buried deep in the river-bed, although most of it must have obviously been carried away by the flood. Accordingly, we bored four holes in the adjacent river-bed and, to our pleasant surprise, found in these bores, at a depth of about 15 meters below the water level (Fig. 40), potsherds characteristic of the PGW Period.

As a result of this massive destruction, the site had to be abandoned. However, it once again came under occupation after a couple of centuries. By now the painted designs on the Painted Grey Ware had disappeared and the fabric too became coarser. But some of the shapes, particularly the dish, continued. However, another de luxe ware emerged. It is known to archaeologists as the Northern Black Polished Ware (NBPW). It

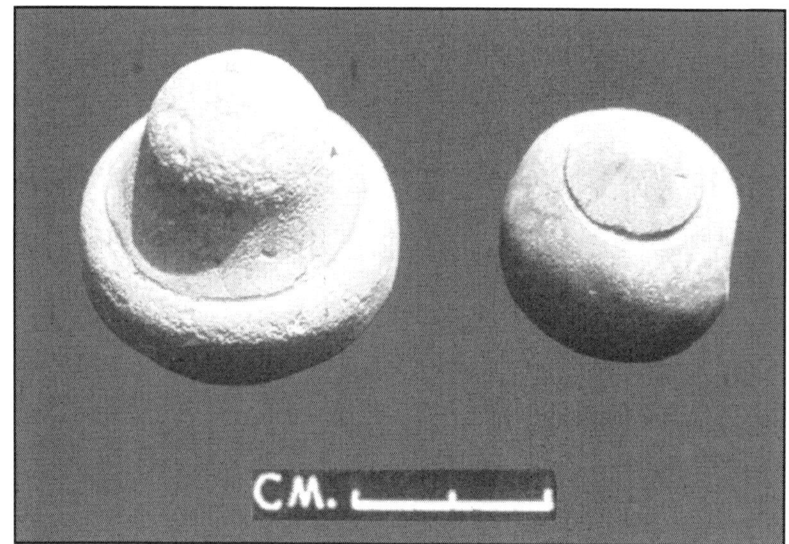

Fig.36: Gamesmen used in the game of *chaupar*, associated with the Painted Grey Ware Culture.

had the same kind of fine grey core as that of the PGW. But the surface had a very fine lustrous slip in a variety of colors: black, indigo, silvery and golden. Shapes in the associated red ware also underwent some change. On the whole, the cultural components of Periods II and III, while showing a change did reflect a generic relationship. This, it may be recalled, was quite in contrast to what happened between Periods I and II.

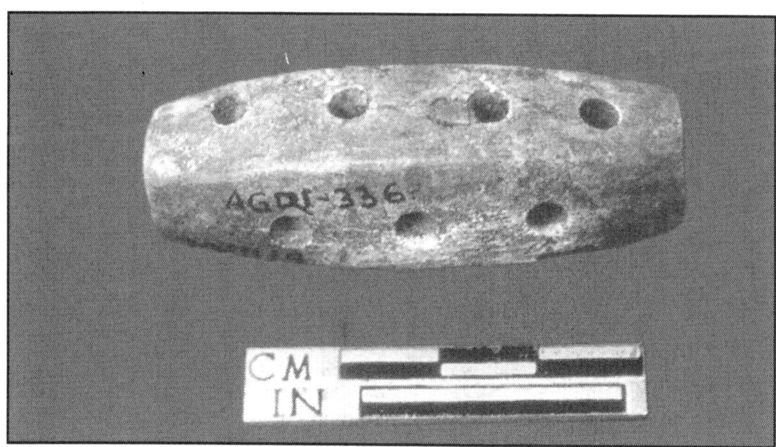

Fig. 37: A dice, used in the game of *chaupar*, associated with the Painted Grey Ware Culture.

Fig. 38: Hastināpura: A heavy flood in the Gaṅgā washed away a considerable portion of the settlement. The man points to the erosional scar left by the flood. Courtesy: ASI

There were many other noticeable changes from Period II to Period III. Thus, in the latter period there was profuse use of kiln-fired bricks, though no doubt mudbricks also continued to be used. With town-planning, a system of public drainage also

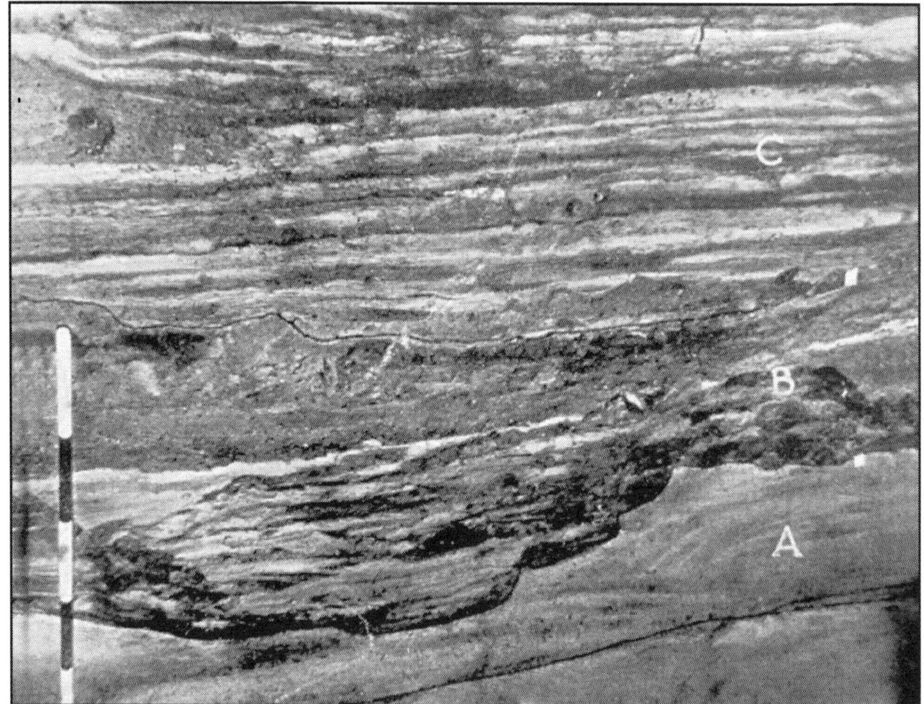

Fig. 39: Hastināpura: A close-up of the deposits near the erosion line. (A), part of the natural soil; (B), dislodged material, re-deposited; and (C), subsequent layers of sand and clay. Courtesy: ASI.

came into being. For soakage of the sullage inside the houses, 'ring-wells' were used (Fig. 41). That the economic level of the people had substantially risen is indicated by the introduction of systems of weights and coinage, both pointing to an augmentation in trade. Indeed, this was the time when the Sixteen States (Ṣoḍaśa Mahājanapadas) had come into being. It was also during this period that the two great religious figures, Buddha and Mahāvira, were born. Nobody is sure about the time when the Brāhmī script originated, but it was during the NBPW times that we do have its clear evidence in the form of the inscriptions of the great emperor Aśoka.

The third occupation at Hastināpura too had a disastrous end. A large-scale fire engulfed the settlement, traces of which were noticed all over the area. As a result, the site was once more abandoned. However, this time too it was not long before the fourth occupation started. But there were some characteristic changes in the cultural equipment. For example, the Northern

Fig. 40: Hastināpura: A view of one of the boreholes dug in the adjacent riverbed. In these bores, potsherds associated with the Painted Grey Ware Culture were found at a depth of nearly 15 meters. Courtesy: ASI.

Black Polished Ware was completely given up and in the red ware too many new shapes made their appearance. There were new types of terracotta figurines, both male and female. The latter were distinguished by their round chummy faces, elaborate hairdo and ornaments, and are generally known as belonging to the 'Śuṅga' style. In the lower levels of this period were found the coins of the rulers of Mathurā (2nd century BCE), followed by those of the Yaudheyas (datable to around the beginning of

Fig. 41: Hastināpura: A view of the structures of Period III. Courtesy: ASI.

the Common Era) in the middle levels and imitation coins of the Kuṣāṇa king Vāsudeva (about the middle of the 3rd century AD) in the upper levels. There is no evidence to indicate how this fourth occupation was abandoned.

However, there was a long gap between the fourth and the fifth (final) occupation of the site. This time the history was laid right in the medieval period. The ceramics were totally different and included two typically distinct glazed wares, one with a whitish sandy core and the other with a red and sturdy one. The former of these is known to have been introduced into India by the incoming Muslim rulers, while the latter seems to have been a local imitation of the former. That the scene was really set in the medieval times is established by the occurrence of a coin of Balban (1266–87 CE) in a middle level. With this period the settlement at the mound came to an end, though there do exist some later Jain temples in the neighbourhood. In fact, an altogether new settlement, planned by the Uttar Pradesh

Government, has come up since we wound up our excavations in the middle of the last century.

D. CHRONOLOGICAL HORIZONS OF THE VARIOUS PERIODS AT HASTINĀPURA

Now to the chronological horizons of the various periods at Hastināpura. As per the details already given above, Period V is datable to *c.* eleventh–fifteenth century CE and Period IV to *c.* second century BCE-third century CE. Since there was a gap between Periods III and IV, the end of the former may reasonably be ascribed to the third century BCE. Up to this point the chronology is based entirely on the evidence of coins. Prior to this we have to fall back on a different kind of evidence.

When in 1951-52 Hastināpura was excavated the Carbon-14 method of dating was not available in India and we had, therefore, to take recourse to what is called 'comparative stratigraphy'. Thus, for dating Period III the main basis was the occurrence, all through the strata, of the Northern Black Polished Ware. Excavations at Bhir Mound in Taxila (now in Pakistan), carried out much earlier, had given a very secure chronology of this ware. From there eighteen specimens of the NBPW had been recovered, of which only one was found within the top 1.8m, while the rest came from depths varying from 1.8 to 3.9m below the surface. And here is the most significant point in the chronology of the NBPW. At a depth of 1.8m below the surface there occurred coins of Alexander **in a mint condition.** It was, therefore, clear that at Bhir Mound the NBPW was essentially pre-Alexandrian, i.e. pre-300 BCE, in date. The 2.1m-thick regular occupational deposit (between 1.8m and 3.9m) would show that at Bhir Mound the NBPW had made its appearance as early as the sixth century BCE. Since the NBPW is essentially a product of the Gaṅgā Valley, its emergence in the valley itself may well go back to the seventh century BCE, or even earlier. With this kind of comparative data, the beginning of Period III at Hastināpura was dated, at the latest, to early sixth century BCE.

Since there was a break of occupation between Periods II and III, and there were also some major elements of cultural evolution from the former to the latter period, as mentioned earlier, the end of Period II is unlikely to have been later than

the eighth century BCE. With this as the upper limit and with over 2 m-thick regular occupation deposits, the site is likely to have been occupied by the Painted Grey Ware people around 1100 BCE.

As already mentioned, there was not only a break of occupation between Periods I and II, but also a fundamental difference between their respective cultural assemblages. Thus, Period I must have well preceded 1200 BCE.

The above chronological assessment of the various periods was made prior to the introduction of the Carbon-14 method of dating in India. It is, however, interesting to note that even after the application of the C-14 method the position has remained by and large the same. In a paper of mine, published in 1980, I have given full details in this regard and those interested are invited to go through this paper. Here, however, we give the gist of it.

There are five radiocarbon dates for Hastināpura, but all these pertain to the **upper levels.** Taking MASCA correction into account, these fall between 720–600+/– 125 BCE and 400+/– 115 BCE. But here is a **major snag** in the application of these radiocarbon dates. **The laboratory report clearly adds a rider that all these samples were mixed with rootlets and hence contaminated.** One is thus left with no choice but to reject these Hastināpura dates, and turn round to the radiocarbon data from other PGW sites in the region. The **middle PGW levels** at Noh, District Bharatpur, Rajasthan, have yielded three C-14 dates. With the application of MASCA correction, these come to: 900+/ - 225 BCE, 805+/- 150 BCE and 745+/- 260 BCE. This would mean that the beginning of the PGW settlement at Noh would go back to the eleventh-twelfth centuries BCE. Similar evidence is provided by the site of Atranjikhera, already referred to earlier. Here, again from a **mid-PGW level** comes a C-14 date of 1025+/ - 110 BCE, which on MASCA correction comes to 1155+/-110 BCE. All the foregoing radiocarbon dates duly support the dating of the PGW settlement at Hastināpura, arrived at in 1952 by the comparative method, namely from *c.* 1100–800 BCE.

As regards the dating of Period I of Hastināpura, thermoluminescence dates from four other Ochre Colour Ware sites in the region, viz. Atranjikhera, Lal Qila, Nasirpur and

Fig. 42: Potsherds of (late) Painted Grey Ware found in the earliest levels of Kauśāmbī.

Jhinjhana, provide collateral evidence. Three of these dates range between 2650 and 2000 BCE, another three between 2000 and 1500 BCE and two in the neighbourhood of 1200 BCE. Thus, the pre-1200 BCE date suggested in 1952 for the OCW occupation at Hastināpura was fairly reasonable, if on the conservative side. Maybe, the settlement dated between 2000 and 1500 BCE, but no one could be too sure of it.

E. THE HASTINĀPURA ARCHAEOLOGICAL EVIDENCE VIS-À-VIS THE *MAHĀBHĀRATA*.

To recapitulate the archaeological data from Hastināpura. Over here five periods of occupation have been found. Of these, the uppermost two (Periods V and IV) do not at all call for consideration in the context of the *Mahābhārata*, since these are far away from the likely date of that episode. Even Period III will have to be ruled out, since its date ranges between *c*. 600 and 300 BCE. Buddha and Mahāvīra lived in the earlier part of this period and, as already stated at the beginning, if the

Mahābhārata episode had any basis in history it had to be pre-Buddha and pre-Mahāvīra.

We are now left with only Periods I and II in the consideration zone. We would have considered the claim of Period I had there not been a very major snag. Of the large number of the Mahābhārata sites enumerated earlier, only two, viz. Hastināpura and Ahichchhatrā, have yielded the Ochre Colour Ware, **the rest have not.** Thus, if the Mahābhārata scene is laid in the OCW period, sites like Mathurā, Indraprastha, Pāṇiprastha, Vṛikaprastha, Vāraṇāvata, Tilaprastha, Virāṭanagara, Kurukṣetra, Kāmpilya, etc. were not at all in existence at that point of time. Could the *Mahābhārata* episode have been enacted without these sites? Obviously not. Thus, the Ochre Colour Ware occupation at Hastināpura cannot claim its association with the Mahābhārata episode.

Thus, in final analysis of the archaeological evidence from Hastināpura, it is only the Painted Grey Ware Culture that qualifies for its association with the Mahābhārata period. In this context it must also be emphasised that all the sites associated with the *Mahābhārata* story have invariably yielded the Painted Grey Ware—a fact which links them together (Fig. 23).

And now we recall the most vital archaeological evidence ever recovered from Hastināpura. It is that of the destruction of the Painted Grey Ware settlement at the site by a flood in the Gaṅgā. In this context, we quote from the *Matsya / Vāyu Purāṇa.* (See Appendix I). The text avers:

Gaṅgayāpahṛite tasmin nagare Nāgasāhvaye
Tyaktvā Nichakṣur nagaram Kauśāmbyām sa nivatsyati

i.e. "When the city of Nāgasāhvya (Hastināpura) is carried away by the Gaṅgā, Nichakṣu will abandon it and dwell in Kauśāmbī."

While the aforementioned archaeological evidence duly confirms the destruction of Hastināpura by a flood in the Gaṅgā, we have to find out if there is any evidence about the shifting of the capital to Kauśāmbī. This could have best come from a contemporary inscription mentioning that event. But, alas! there is no such inscription. As is well known, we do not yet have any inscription dating prior to the fourth century BCE. Then, is there

any other kind of evidence which may throw light on the issue? The situation is not so bad as it would appear to be. Here again archaeology comes to our rescue. In the lowest levels of Kauśāmbī have been found potsherds of the Painted Grey Ware (Fig. 42). The Kauśāmbī PGW, however, does not present the ware at its peak, as it does in the middle levels at Hastināpura. The Kauśāmbī specimens bear only simple linear designs but are bereft of the more variegated ones like sigmas, swastikas, chain of spirals, etc. (Fig. 26). The texture is also slightly coarser. But these are the very features which have their own significance. They represent the decadent stage of the ware and thus provide a significant link between the end of Hastināpura and the beginning of Kauśāmbī.

F. THE DATE OF THE MAHĀBHĀRATA WAR ON THE BASIS OF ARCHAEOLOGICAL-CUM-LITERARY EVIDENCE

The Kauśāmbī PGW levels are bereft of any NBPW, which appeared only later. Further, since the emergence of the NBPW in the Gaṅgā Valley is likely to go back to the seventh-eighth century BCE, the PGW levels at Kauśāmbī may well be dated to *c.* 800 BCE. Thus, put together, the archaeological evidence from Hastināpura and Kauśāmbī would show that the flood and the consequent desertion of the former site, and the establishment of a settlement at the latter can safely be placed around 800 BCE. It may be recalled that the flood occurred during the reign of Nichakṣu who was the fifth ruler in succession from Parīkṣit and the latter, in turn, ascended the throne of Hastināpura immediately after the Mahābhārata War. Thus, the war itself may be deemed to have taken place around 900 BCE.

The above-mentioned date of the Mahābhārata War, arrived at on archaeological grounds, may now be cross-checked with literary evidence. The *Vāyu Purāṇa* says that after Nichakṣu there were nineteen rulers at Kauśāmbī before Udayana came to the throne (see Appendix I). While sceptics may doubt the historicity of the earlier kings of Kauśāmbī, even they would not deny that there did exist a king called Udayana, since his contemporaneity with Buddha has never been questioned. It was he who invited Buddha to visit Kauśāmbī and the latter

duly responded. Buddha passed away in 487 or 483 BCE. Thus, Udayana can well be taken to have ruled around 500 BCE.

Now comes the most baffling aspect of the issue: How many years did actually elapse between the time of Nichakṣu and that of Udayana? And the answer at once falls in the realm of subjectivity. There have been a number of estimates for the average reign per ruler. There are those who hold it to have been 33 years or even 37, but most sober scholars regard it to be an overestimation. There are, however, other moderate estimates which deserve consideration. While A.L. Basham puts it at 19 years, Pargiter does it at 18. However, even while recommending the estimate of 18, Pargiter (1962: 181-82) inserts a caveat:

> I have examined 14 series of dynasties from 20 to 30 kings in various eastern and western countries; the longest average just exceeded 24 years in one case, the shortest was about 12 and the average of all was 19; but the average was higher in western countries and lower in eastern countries. Hence the medium average for these contemporary eastern dynasties must be taken something less than 19 and 18 will be a fair, **even liberal** estimate. (Emphasis added.)

Like Pargiter, I thought of doing my own exercise; and since the problem is related specifically to India, I thought of examining it in the light of Indian dynasties whose dates are already well known. Thus, to begin with, I took up the Muslim rulers of Delhi. Qutbuddin Aibak was the first one to occupy the throne of Delhi after defeating Prithvi Raj Chauhan. The last Muslim ruler of Delhi was Bahadur Shah Zafar whom the British ousted. Altogether there were 47 rulers from the first to the last, and the total duration of their reigns was 652 years. This gives an average of 13.9 years per ruler. When this average was presented to scholars, they were not happy with it, arguing that since there were many coups and killings in the various Muslim dynasties, the average is bound to be low. But they forgot that while some of the kings may have ruled for only a couple of years, there were others like Akbar (1556–1605 CE) and Aurangzeb (1658–1707 CE) who ruled for very long time. But this did not satisfy them. So I took up the ancient Hindu dynasties. Of these, the Guptas gave the highest average, which stood at 17.6 years. On the other hand, the Kaṇvas yielded an average of only 10.5 years and the Śuṅgas that of 11.2. The Mauryas stood in-between. On piecing together the averages of all the Hindu dynasties whose reigns are well fixed, it was observed that their overall average was still a little less than 14 years per ruler. **Thus, in the Indian context, whether medieval or ancient, the safe and reliable average would be around 14 years. Please see the Table below:**

An exercise in computing average years per ruler

S.No.	*Dynasty*	*Number of Rulers*	*Total Duration*	*Average per ruler*
1.	Maurya	10	137	13.7
2.	Śuṅga	10	112	11.2
3.	Kaṇva	4	45	10.5
4.	Sātavāhana	19	274	14.4
5.	Gupta	10	176	17.6
6.	Muslim Rulers of Delhi	47	652	13.9
			Total	81.3
		Average of Averages	=	81.3÷6 13.55 years

This average of 13.55 years per ruler may be rounded off to 14 or even 15 years. Multiplying this figure with the number of rulers that preceded Udayana back to the Mahābhārata War, viz. 24 (19 from Udayana to Nichakṣu and 5 further back to the War), the total period that elapsed would be 15 x 24 = 360 years. Since, as already stated, Udayana was ruling around 500 BCE, the date of the Mahābhārata War would work out to around 860 BCE. It would, however, be too presumptuous to stick to a precise figure like this, and all that one can say is that even the literary-cum-historical analysis supports the date of *c*. 900 BCE for the war, arrived at on the basis of the combined archaeological evidence from Hastināpura and Kauśāmbī.

G. OTHER DATES EXAMINED

But a doubt lurks in my mind if such a late date would ever please the orthodox school of scholars, since to them the Mahābhārata War is very 'hoary', going back to 3102 BCE. The

reason why they regard it to be so early is that an inscription at Aihole, in Karnataka State, dated to Śaka Era 556, i.e. AD 634–35, mentions that 3735 years had elapsed since the Mahābhārata War. One wonders where the author of the Aihole inscription got his information from, suddenly 3735 years after the event.

In recent years there has been a great spurt in harnessing the astronomical data given in the *Mahābhārata* for dating the war. In April 2012 an International Conference on "The *Mahābhārata*: Its Historicity, Antiquity, Evolution and Impact on Civilization" was held in Delhi at which Professor Narhar Achar of University of Memphis (USA) presented a paper on "Historicity of Mahābhārata War: Astronomical Methods using Planetarium Software." By using the planetarium software, he arrived at 3067 BCE for the war. At the same time, he listed the findings of some other scholars, using astronomical data, whose conclusions were at great variance from his own, viz. 1478 BCE and 2559 BCE.

My problem with the date provided by the Aihole inscription (namely 3102 BCE) and that by Professor Achar (namely 3067 BCE) is as follows.

As the archaeological data indicate, in 3102/3067 BCE none of the Mahābhārata-associated-sites such as Hastināpura, Mathurā, Pāṇiprastha, Tilprastha, Vārṇāvata, Kurukṣetra, etc. ever existed. They came up nearly 2000 years later. Can we then enact the *Mahābhārata* story without these sites providing the necessary stage? Further, if we accept 3102/3067 BCE as the date of the Mahābhārata War, the average reign of the 24 rulers between the end of the War and Udayana (500 BCE), referred to above, would be: 3102/3067 minus 500, divided by 24= 108 years. This is very much more than even the average lifespan of a person, not to speak of the period of a reign! Please give the matter a serious thought.

However, there are a few other dates which do call for consideration: for example, 1424 BCE (proposed by K.P. Jayaswal), 1400 BCE (A.S. Altekar), 950 BCE (F.E. Pargiter) and ninth century BCE (H.C. Raychaudhury). As regards the first two dates, it may be recalled that this was the time up to which the Copper Hoard-cum-Ochre Colour Ware Culture may have persisted. But then, with the exception of Hastināpura and Ahichchhatrā, the remains of this Culture have not been found at any of the other sites figuring in the Mahābhārata story. Also conversely, no other

Copper Hoard-cum-Ochre Colour Ware site, such as Nasirpur, Bahadrabad, Jhinjhana, Saifai, Bisauli, to name just a few, find any mention in the *Mahābhārata.* How can then one correlate the two?

We are now left with 950 BCE (Pargiter) and ninth century BCE (Raychaudhury). Pargiter's dating is based on the average of 18 years per reign. However, he himself thought this average to be 'liberal', and, as shown earlier, a more reasonable average would be 14-15 years. Thus, even Pargiter's dating is a little off the mark. Raychaudhury's dating has an additional merit. He steers clear of the oft-debated Paurāṇic data and uses completely independent evidence, viz. that of the later Vedic texts. Thus, basing his arguments on the teacher-disciple sequence given in these texts, and working backwards from the known ones, he observes that the time of Parīkṣit, who ascended the Hastināpura throne immediately on the conclusion of the Mahābhārata War, is likely to have been somewhere in the ninth century BCE. And this is precisely what our archaeological evidence suggests.

Before we wind up this discussion on the date of the Mahābhārata War, one more aspect of the issue also needs to be examined. In recent years a late Haṛappan site, encroached upon by the sea, has been discovered at Dwārakā in Gujarat and it has been claimed that this is the Dwārakā where Kṛiṣṇa lived in the later part of his life. Thus, according to this view, the Mahābhārata episode must have taken place sometime at the beginning of the second millennium BCE. However, there are two snags in this argument. In the first place, there were many successive settlements at Dwārakā, ranging from the late Harappan times all the way up to the medieval period and there is no sound basis to identify any particular settlement, to the exclusion of the others, as having been associated with the time of Kṛiṣṇa. Secondly, and this is no less important a point to be considered, during the occupancy of this particular Dwārakā which is supposed to have been of the time of Kṛiṣṇa, namely at the beginning of the second millennium BCE, none of the key sites associated with the Mahābhārata story, even Mathurā from where Kṛiṣṇa himself hailed, was in existence. What then is the validity of this particular Dwārakā **without there having been any contemporary Mathurā?**

CHAPTER 8

Don't Throw the Baby Out with the Bath Water

Do we have any contemporary inscription to establish the historicity of the *Mahābhārata* and/or of Kṛiṣṇa—a principal actor in that epic? The answer is a frank 'No'. But then does it mean that the absence of a contemporary inscription negates the historicity either of the *Mahābhārata* or of Kṛiṣṇa? We must recall the age-old saying that "absence of evidence is no evidence of absence". Further, let it also be remembered that we do not have any contemporary inscription to vouchsafe the historicity of either the Buddha or Mahāvīra. Some people try to mislead us by saying that there is a contemporary inscription to establish the historicity of the Buddha. In this respect they refer to the Lumbini Pillar Inscription. But surely that is not contemporary with the Buddha. It was put up **nearly 300 years later** by Ashoka

who happened to visit that place and was evidently told by the local inhabitants that the Buddha was born there, when his mother was on way to her parents' home. And let it also be understood that the local people who were Ashoka's source of information were not eyewitnesses to the fact that Buddha was born there. They must have learnt about this event from their parents who, in turn, must have learnt about it from their parents, and so on. Thus, at least twelve generations were involved in passing the story by word of mouth. Can we then really call this kind of evidence **'contemporary'?** And the position in respect of an inscription contemporary with Mahāvīra is much worse. The earliest inscription referring to him is more than half a millennium later. Thus, to insist on having a contemporary inscription would not be the right approach to establish the historicity of a person or an event. We should, I believe, pool together all kinds of evidences and then make a holistic judgement.

In Chapter 6 we tried to piece together the evidence of ancient non-epic literature. First we took up texts like the *Atharvaveda Saṁhitā, Aitareya Brāhmaṇa* and *Bṛihadāraṇyaka Upaniṣad,* which are Vedic texts, in no way under the influence of the *Mahābhārata.* Thereafter we cited the evidence of Pāṇini's *Aṣṭādhyāyī* and Kauṭilya's *Arthaśāstra,* which are purely secular texts, again, in no way influenced by the *Mahābhārata.* Thus, the evidence of these non-epic texts is totally independent and hence trustworthy in respect of the historicity or otherwise of that epic.

To recall very briefly, the *Atharvaveda Saṁhitā* mentions King (*rājā*) Parīkṣit and his kingdom (*rāṣṭra*), while *Aitareya Brāhmaṇa* refers to Janamejaya as the son of Parīkṣit. The *Bṛihadāraṇyaka Upaniṣad* states that the fate of the descendants of Parīkṣit was discussed in the court of Janaka, the emperor of Videha.

Pāṇini's *Aṣṭādhyāyī*, in one of its *sūtras*, refers jointly to Vāsudeva (Kṛiṣṇa) and Arjuna. The *Arthaśāstra* of Kauṭilya minces no words and states that Janamejaya was doomed because of his wrath against the Brāhmaṇas; so also Duryodhana, who refused to part with even a bit of his kingdom, because of vanity.

It would thus be seen that most of the important personages of the *Mahābhārata*, namely Kṛiṣṇa, Arjuna, Duryodhana, Parīkṣit

and Janamejaya, find mention in **texts which are quite independent of the *Mahābhārata*.** This should leave no doubt that these are indeed historical figures and not figments of somebody's imagination.

The excavation at Hastināpura has yielded evidence which is of great significance. Over here the Painted Grey Ware settlement was destroyed, sometime in the ninth century BCE, by a huge flood in the Gaṅgā. As mentioned earlier (p. 83), the Purāṇas state that during the reign of Nichakṣu a flood washed away Hastināpura, as a result of which the capital was shifted to Kauśāmbī. The excavation at Kauśāmbī has shown that the settlement over there began with a late stage of the Painted Grey Ware. Thus, though there is no inscription to prove the shifting of the capital from Hastināpura to Kauśāmbī, the archaeological evidence does establish a connection between the end of Hastināpura and the beginning of Kauśāmbī. Further, the date for the abandonment, because of a heavy flood, of the PGW settlement at Hastināpura tallies very well with the date arrived at on the basis of the duration of the reigns of the rulers from Udayana back to Nichakṣu, in whose time the flood took place. This correlation gives us a date around 900 BCE for the Mahābhārata War.

It would thus be seen that the evidences of non-epic literature as well as that of archaeology duly establish the historicity of the principal personages and of the main events and sites associated with the *Mahābhārata*. In other words, the epic has a basis in history, though no doubt its bulk consists of subsequent interpolations some of which are likely to be as late as the 4th century CE, since these refer to the Hūṇas who appeared on the Indian scene around that century. It is also a well-known fact that literature mirrors the contemporary features of the material culture. Thus, the description of the buildings and palaces and of the developed weapons of war may reflect what was there in the early centuries of the Common Era and not of what obtained around 900 BCE when the war seems to have taken place. In this context, it may also be recalled that the poor *Jaya* consisting of only 8,800 verses was first expanded to the *Bhārata* of 24,000 verses, and finally blown into the colossus of the *Mahābhārata* of 1,00,000 verses. Let not the skinny core of the text be discarded because of the subsequent fatty overgrowth. It has been well said: "Don't throw the baby out with the bath water!"

APPENDIX I

From Parīkṣit to Udayana

F.E. Pargiter, the renowned scholar of the Purāṇas, gives a composite text from the *Matsya* and *Vāyu Purāṇas* relating to the Paurava Dynasty (*The Purāṇa Text of the Dynasties of the Kali Age*, Delhi: Deep Publications, Reprint, 1975, pp. 3-8), which is reproduced below. Where there are two columns, the one on the left is from the *Matsya Purāṇa* and that on the right, from the *Vāyu*.

Abhimanyoḥ Parīkṣit *tu*	*Uttarāyām tu Vairāṭyām*
Putraḥ para-puraṁ-jayaḥ	***Parikṣit Abhimanyūjaḥ***
Janamejayaḥ *Parikṣitaḥ*	*Parikṣitas tu dāyādo*
Putraḥ paramadhārmikaḥ	*rāj-āsīj* ***Janamejayaḥ***
Janamejayāch ***Chhatānīkas***	*tasya putraḥ* ***Śatānīko***
tasmāj jajñe sa vīryvān	*balvān satya-vikramaḥ*

putro ***'śvamedhadatto*** *'bhūch Chhatānīkasya vīryavān*

putro 'śvamedhadattād vai jātaḥ para-puraṁ-jayaḥ
***Adhisīmakṛiṣṇo** dharm-ātmā sāmprataṁ yo mahā-yaśāḥ*
*Adhisīmakṛiṣṇa-putro **Nichakṣur** bhavitā nṛipaḥ*
Gaṇgay-āpahṛite tasmin nagare Nāgasāhvaye
Tyakvā Nicakṣur nagaram Kauśāmbyām sa nivatsyati
Bhaviṣy-āṣṭau sutās tasya mahā-bala-parākramaḥ
***Bhūrir** jyeṣṭhaḥ sutas tasya* *bhaviṣyad **Uṣṇas** tat-putra*
*tasya **Chitrarathaḥ** smṛitaḥ* *Uṣṇāch **Chitrarathaḥ** smṛitaḥ*
***Śuchidrathaś** Chitrarathād **Vṛiṣṇimāms** cha Śuchidrathāt*
*Vṛṣṇimataḥ **Suṣeṇas** cha bhaviṣyati śuchir nṛipaḥ*
*Tasmāt Suṣeṇād bhavitā **Sunītho** nāma pārthivaḥ*
***Ruchaḥ** Sunīthād bhavitā **Nṛichakṣur** bhavitā tataḥ*
*Nṛichakṣuṣas tu dāyādo bhavitā vai **Sukhībalaḥ***
*Sukhībala-sutaś chāpi bhāvī rājā **Pariplavaḥ***
*Pariplava-sutas chāpi bhavitā **Sunayo** nṛipaḥ*
***Medhāvī** tasya dāyādo bhaviṣyati narādhipaḥ*
*Medhavinaḥ sutaś chāpi bhaviṣyati **Nṛipañjayaḥ***
***Durvo** bhāvyaḥ sutas tasya **Tigmātmā** tasya chātmajah*
*Tigmad **Bṛihadratho** bhāvyo **Vasudāno** Bṛihadrathāt*
*Vasudānāch **Chhatānīko** bhaviṣy-**Odayanas** tataḥ*
*Bhaviṣyate ch-Odayanād viro rājā **Vahīnaraḥ***
*Vahīnarātmajaś chaiva **Daṇḍapāṇir** bhaviṣyati*
*Daṇḍāpaner **Nirāmitro** Nirāmitrāt tu **Kṣemakaḥ***
pañcaviṁśa nṛipā hyete bhaviṣyāḥ purūvaṁśajāḥ
atrānuvaṁsa-śloko yaṁ gīto vipraiḥ purātanaiḥ
brahma-kṣatrasya yo yonir vaṁśo devarṣi-satkṛitaḥ
Kṣemakam prāpya rājānaṁ saṁsthām prāpsyati vai Kalau
Ity eṣa Pauravo vaṁśo yathāvad anukīrtitaḥ
dhīmataḥ Pāṇḍūputrasya Arjunasya mahātmanaḥ

APPENDIX II

Ballads have a Field Day, Even Today

In the very first paragraph of Chapter I, we mentioned that the *Mahābhārata* swelled from a small beginning of 8,800 verses (called the *Jaya)* to 24,000 verses (called the *Bhārata*) and thence to its present whopping figure of 1,00,000 verses (called the *Mahābhārata*). How this process of interpolation and inflation takes place can be exemplified by something very recent, of which the present writer has had a personal experience.

It was January 1954. I was travelling from Calcutta to Delhi on an official visit. Piercing the fog of the morning, my train, Kalka Mail, steamed into Allahabad railway station. Suddenly I saw thousands and thousands of people jostling with one another on all the platforms the station has. They were desperately trying to get out of Allahabad and never bothered about either buying a ticket or about the class of compartment they were getting into. About fifty people forced their way into my small compartment as well. In about ten minutes the train steamed off. I really could not make out what had happened and the incomers too were so horrified that except for occasional shrieks nothing came out from their mouths. They were completely exhausted and aghast and detrained in batches as their respective stations arrived.

By the evening I too reached my destination. After dinner, I switched on the radio. (There was no television—at least in India—at that time.) In came the news that scores of people had died and hundreds injured in the Kumbha Mela at Allahabad. Lakhs of them had gathered to have a dip in the holy Gaṅgā on this occasion. Amongst the people who had assembled were Nāgā Sādhūs (naked mendicants). The news had it that when these Sāhdūs were moving in, their elephants ran amuck and a few persons were run over. Out of fear, those nearby started running away. This set in a chain reaction and without even pausing to ascertain the extent of the problem, the entire crowd started running helter-skelter. In the great melee that followed, hundreds of men, women and children were trampled over. Many breathed their last on the spot, while hundreds got severely injured. Later, when the crowd somewhat thinned down, police vans took the injured to hospitals and the dead to mortuaries for subsequent identification and cremation. During the pandemonium, the criminals had a field day. They not only robbed the women folk of their jewellery, but even molested some of them. Most of these details came out in the newspapers the next morning. Later on, the government, as usual, instituted an enquiry, and so on.

That was 1954. Some thirty years later, we were excavating at Śṛiṅgaverapura, near Allahabad. We had the practice of sharing weekend evenings with the workmen, with a lot of dance and music. On one of the evenings I had a real surprise. One of the workers, playing on his *khartāls*, sang to us a ballad which narrated in great detail the Kumbha Mela incident referred to above. Later on, I learnt that, besides this Śṛiṅgaverapura version, there were two others, created by the ballad-singers respectively from Jhusi and Daraganj. While the basic fact, viz. that there occurred such and such incident at Allahabad on the

occasion of the Kumbha Mela in 1954, constituted the core of all the three versions, each one had a lot of its own *mircha-masālā* (spicy additions and interpolations) so much so that one did not know which one to believe. When such deviations and distortions can take place in the narration of an event which took place before our very eyes and which was also immediately reported through electronic and print media, no wonder that the nucleus of the *Mahābhārata* story, which must have been sung in the form a small ballad to begin with, swelled out of all proportions into perhaps one of the largest poetic narratives ever produced by mankind. The simple lesson is that we ought to be discerning enough to separate the wheat from the chaff.

Bibliography

Banerjee, P., 1973. *Early Indian Religions,* Delhi, Vikas Publishing House Pvt. Ltd.

——, 1978. *The Life of Krishṇa in Indian Art,* New Delhi, National Museum.

Das, Asok Kumar, 2005. *Paintings of the Razmnāmā: The Book of War,* Kolkata, Birla Academy of Art and Culture, Mapin Publishing.

Gaur, R.C., 1983. *Excavations at Atranjikhera,* Delhi, Motilal Banarsidass.

Joshi, J.P., 1993. *Excavation at Bhagwanpura 1975-76,* New Delhi, Archaeological Survey of India.

Lal, B.B., 1954 and 1955. Excavations at Hastināpura and Other Explorations in the Upper Gaṅgā and Sutlej Basins 1950-52, *Ancient India,* Nos. 10 and 11.

——, 1980. Did the Painted Grey Ware Continue up to the Mauryan Times? *Puratattva,* 9: 64-80.

——, 2008. *Rama: His Historicity, Mandir and Setu,* New Delhi, Aryan Books International.

Madhavananda, Swami, 1965. The *Bṛihadāraṇyaka Upaniṣad*, Calcutta, Advaita Ashrama.

Mahadevan, T.P., 2011. Three Rails of the Mahābhārata Text Tradition, in *Journal of Vaishnava Studies*, 19(2): 23-69.

Malaviya, Sudhakar (ed.), 1983. *The Aitareya Brāhmaṇa of the Ṛigveda*, 2 vols. Varanasi, Tata Printing Works.

Manavalan, A.A., 2004. Tamil Versions of the *Mahābhārata* and Studies on the Tamil Versions. In Ajay Mitra Shastri (ed.) *Mahābhārata: The End of an Era (Yugānta)*, pp. 326-52. Shimla, Indian Institute of Advanced Study and New Delhi, Aryan Books Internatonal.

Pargiter, F.E., 1962. *Ancient Indian Historical Tradition.* Delhi (reprint).

——, 1975. *The Purāṇa Text of the Dynasties of the Kali Age*, Delhi, Deep Publications (reprint).

Ramesh, K.V., 2004. The *Mahābhārata* in Inscriptions. In Ajay Mitra Shastri (ed.) *Mahābhārata: The End of an Era (Yugānta)*, pp. 298-313. Shimla, IIAS and New Delhi, Aryan Books International.

Raychaudhuri, Hemchandra, 1972. *Political History of Ancient India.* University of Calcutta.

Ritti, Shrinivas, 2004. Mahābhārata in Early Kannad Literature. In Ajay Mitra Shastri (ed.) *Mahābhārata: The End of an Era (Yugānta)*, pp. 353-66. Shimla, IIAS and New Delhi, Aryan Books International.

Roveda, Vittorio, 2003. *Sacred Angkor: The Carved Reliefs of Angkor Wat*, (with photographs by Jaro Poncar), Weatherhill Inc., 41, Monroe Turnpike, Trumbull, CT 06611.

Shamasastry, R., 1960. *Kauṭilya's Arthaśāstra* (in English), Mysore, Mysore Printing and Publishing House.

Shastri, Ajay Mitra (ed.), 2004. *Mahābhārata: The End of an Era (Yugānta).* Shimla, Indian Institute of Advanced Study and New Delhi, Aryan Books International.

Shastri, Udayavira, 1988. *Kauṭalīya Arthaśāstra* (in Hindi), New Delhi, Meharchand Lachhmandas Publications.

Sircar, Dines Chandra. 1965. *Select Inscriptions Bearing on Indian History and Civilization*, Vol. I, University of Calcutta.

——, 1983. *Select Inscriptions Bearing on Indian History and Civilization*, Vol. II, Delhi, Motilal Banarsidass.

Sukthankar, Vishnu S., 1933. *The Adiparvan* (along with the Prolegomena) of the critically edited *Mahābhārata* (CE), Poona (Pune), Bhandarkar Oriental Research Institute.

Index

THE BOOK

To the faithful, everything mentioned in the *Mahābhārata* is true to the very letter, whereas the skeptic holds that the epic is nothing more than a mere figment of imagination. How, then, can one ascertain the truth? It is here that archaeology comes to our rescue.

In 1951-52, Professor B.B. Lal excavated the key-site of Hastināpura, situated on the bank of the Gaṅgā, in Meerut district of Uttar Pradesh. Over here he encountered in the lower levels a settlement which was distinguished by a characteristic pottery called the Painted Grey Ware, assignable to circa 1100-800 BCE. This PGW Culture has since been discovered at **all the Mahābhārata sites—a feature which binds them together**.

Further, the excavation revealed that a heavy flood in the Gaṅgā destroyed a considerable portion of the Painted Grey Ware settlement at Hastināpura. This archaeological evidence is duly corroborated by the *Vāyu Purāṇa* which states: "when the city of Hastināpura is carried away by the Gaṅgā, Nichkṣu will abandon it and dwell in Kauśāmbī."

The shifting of the capital from Hastināpura to Kauśāmbī is, in turn, supported by the fact that in the lowest levels of Kauśāmbī has been encountered the same kind of degenerated Painted Grey Ware as had begun to appear at Hastināpura prior to its destruction by the flood.

Thus, the combined evidence of archaeology and literature duly establishes that **the *Mahābhārata* is not a figment of imagination but has a basis in historical reality.** At the same time, it is on record that the epic underwent eleven-time inflation 8,800 to 1,00,000 verseshence it is difficult to separate the wheat from the chaff. **But let not the precious wheat be thrown away with the chaff**.